Sorting Things Out

Sorting Things Out

GEORGE F. DOLE

J. Appleseed & Co.
San Francisco

Editor: *Steve Koke*

Cover & book design: *DBA Design & Illustration, San Carlos, CA*

Designer: *Lorene Ray Lederer*

Text set in 11/14.5 Garamond. Accents set in Stone Sans.

CONTENTS
—

EDITOR'S PREFACE

The Rev. Dr. George Dole is one of the most widely admired Swedenborgian scholars in the world. His writings and talks are noted for their profound insight, penetrating research, and engagingly direct and elegant style.

He was ordained into the ministry of the Swedenborgian Church in 1960 and served the Cambridge, Massachusetts, parish for thirteen years. In the meantime, he took his Ph.D. (in Assyriology) at Harvard in 1965 and began a long career on the faculty of the Swedenborg School of Religion. He has an impressive list of publications and film scripts to his credit and has become a leading translator of the works of Emanuel Swedenborg from the Latin. Seemingly never too busy, he is currently a director of the Swedenborg Foundation.

George Dole's talks (lectures, sermons, discussion presentations) enjoy an honored reputation among Swedenborgians for their scholarly creativity and tight construction. These perishable works of theology became in many cases the workbench from which a more general spiritual philosophy developed. It was decided, therefore, to publish a diverse sampling from this rich largesse. Thirty-two of the best, covering the last decade or so, were chosen from a large collection for this book. The final choices were not easy; the pieces judged to be most suitable for the book were by far the most numerous.

The title *Sorting Things Out* refers to an elemental skill in dealing with life. The powerful art of sorting through tangled issues until some of heaven's light breaks through all by itself is unfortunately not often seen. It is our impression that this subtle skill is what most persistently underlies George's thought.

These gracefully written talks on theological ideas, social issues, and the delicate art of living help us live with spiritual integrity in today's complicated world.

— *Steve Koke*
Grass Valley, California

Who's Doing What
Around Here?

One of the major themes in the history of Christian doctrine centers in a tension between—in the terms most common in non-Swedenborgian Christian theology—"law" and "grace." My colleague Bob Kirven uses a pendulum model to show how the emphasis shifted back and forth over the centuries, with relatively few theologians finding a balance between the two.

The central question involved is simply stated. "On whom does my salvation depend, God or me?" "Law" theologians would say that it depends on me. The pivotal decisions are in my hands. The Sacred Scriptures reveal the laws of life, and I must follow them if I am to be admitted to heaven. This view underlies the Catholic system of catalogued sins, confession, and penance. "Grace" theologians insist that we cannot save ourselves, that only God has the power to deliver us from evil. One extreme form of this is Calvin's doctrine of predestination, which maintains that God alone decides who is to be saved.

Swedenborg is one of the few theologians who manage to maintain that there is essential truth in both of these positions. Yes, we have no power to save ourselves, and yes, we must do the work of repentance and reformation of life if regeneration is to happen. This was an important enough point that he found a concise way of expressing it and used it repeatedly—that we are to shun evils as if of ourselves, and at the same time are to acknowledge that it is actually the Lord who is doing the work.

I would suggest that our understanding of this familiar principle ought to change, to deepen, in the course of our lives, and that we might well look at that understanding as a kind of index to our current spiritual state. What is involved is our present working relationship with the Lord, and in our own personal histories, there is likely to be a kind of pendulum movement like that which Bob Kirven outlines in the history of Christian doctrine. There are times when, quite appropriately, we feel that everything is up to us, that we have to haul up our own socks and fight our own fights. There are other times when, with equal appropriateness, we feel utterly powerless, and can only hope for the Lord's deliverance. When the pendulum is at the point of balance, we find ourselves doing our best with a consciousness that our "independence" is only an appearance.

To me, one of the most persuasive arguments in favor of maintaining the tension between law and grace is to be found in the "Twelve Steps" programs, with Alcoholics Anonymous as the first and best-known example. Step one reads (in one adaptation), "We admitted we were powerless over [our addiction], and that our lives had become unmanageable." Step three reads, "We made a decision to turn our will and our lives over to the care of the Higher Power, as we understood it." Step six reads, "We were entirely ready to have the Higher Power remove these defects of character." These steps in particular focus on "grace," on the recognition that we cannot change ourselves. But step four reads, "We made a searching and fearless moral inventory of ourselves." Step nine reads, "We made direct amends to people we had harmed wherever possible, except when to do so would injure them or others." Step eleven reads, "We sought through prayer and meditation to improve our conscious contact with the Higher Power as we understood it, praying only for knowledge of its will for us and the power to carry that out." And step twelve reads, "Having had a spiritual awakening as the result of these steps, we tried to carry this message to others and to practice these principles in all our affairs." These steps assume that there is something we not only can but must do.

The persuasiveness of this for me does not lie in its theoretical coherence or its accord with Swedenborgian doctrines. It lies rather in the fact that it works. Of all the approaches to addiction that have been designed and tried, this is the most effective. Because of it, literally millions of alcoholics have lived in sobriety. It is also worth mentioning another rare fact, namely that A. A. has endured as an organization without losing sight of its essential purpose and without losing its integrity. It has not followed the apparently inevitable pattern of organizations—starting with idealistic missionary zeal, and by the third generation becoming an institution primarily concerned with its own survival. Churches in general, including our own, can hardly make that claim.

But I hasten to add that A. A. has one major advantage over the church. Alcohol is an identifiable substance, and its abuse has readily observable effects. Alcoholics are people who are literally unable to control their drinking, so that drinking consistently impairs their functioning as human beings. There is a clear, definable behavioral problem to deal with. The enemy is out in the open.

The same cannot be said of "sin" in general, and it can be observed that members of A. A. often have real difficulty with the last clause of the twelfth step— 'to practice these principles in all our affairs." It is not so easy to say that I am powerless to heal this relationship with another human being as to say that I am powerless to control my drinking. The relationship is a complex of many factors, and many facets of my own being are involved in it. Or to take it one step further, it would not be easy to design a program for "Egotists Anonymous," because egotism can take so many different forms.

I suspect, then, that churches fall so readily into institutionalism because the central task is such a difficult and elusive one. If the enemy is "evil," then we know in advance that we may surmount one form of it only to have it surface again in a different form. By self-discipline, we overcome a troublesome habit and find ourselves prey to self-righteousness. We find self-satisfaction in moments of humility. This is in fact the inherent weakness in too strong a focus on law, on our part of the process. It centers our consciousness on what we must conceive to be our own strength. It is much simpler to support the church and to abide by its behavioral principles.

I have not done an exhaustive search of our collateral literature, but I am not aware of much that deals directly with the "as if of self" issue, which disappoints me. It seems almost as though our church has really taken the side of the law, with an intellectual bow to grace. That is, we are satisfied if we make a genuine effort to lead good and constructive lives, and if we know from doctrine that our strength to do so is a gift from the Lord. We do not talk much about the experience of powerlessness that shifts this doctrine from our heads to our hearts, that moves us from "information about" to "personal acquaintance with."

I trust it is obvious that this "personal acquaintance with" cannot be transmitted in a lecture. There is no substitute for doing our very best and discovering that it is totally useless. Steps two through eleven are quite pointless without step one— "we admitted that we were powerless." And I cannot emphasize strongly enough that we must give it our best shot first. There is a part of us that wants to believe that we really could overcome if we put forth our best effort, and nothing but the failure of our best effort will still that voice.

Anything else, in fact, would be a cop-out. We would be saying, in effect, "Lord, I know I don't really need you, that I could handle this on my own, but it would be so much quicker and easier if you would just take care of it for me." This is tantamount to asking the Lord to help us maintain the illusion that we ourselves have power over our evils. It is telling the Lord that we do not actually want to know the truth about ourselves. It is evading the central question of our existence.

Since a lecture is not a substitute for the experience, then, what can a lecture do? Perhaps it can help us understand the necessity of the experience, so that we are less inclined to avoid or postpone it. For the Lord's providence guards above all our essential freedom and will not force us into admissions that we are unwilling to make. This means that it may be helpful to look at a wider view of our own natures, to confront some of the illusions that make it hard for us to face the fact of our powerlessness.

For me, much of the most practical and relevant information about this is gathered in *Divine Love and Wisdom*. This is where Swedenborg gets down to the very basics that are determinant in all situations in all ages. This is where, for example, he talks about direct and indirect influx, and that leads us in some surprising directions.

The basic picture is simple. Everything that exists is maintained in its existence by two forces, one acting from the inside and one acting from the outside. At this moment, the pressure inside our bodies nicely matches the air pressure from the outside, so we are comfortable. If we drive up Mount Washington, we will experience discomfort as the outside pressure lessens, until the inside pressure adjusts.

This is equally true of us as spiritual beings. We are maintained in our humanity by the intersection of two flows. One is the inflow of life directly from the Lord into what Swedenborg calls "the inmost," and the other is the flow of spiritual forces from the Lord through our spiritual and natural surroundings. There is a story in *Heaven and Hell* about a spirit who believed he was independent of other spirits. It tells how the inner communication with other spirits was cut off, and how he became infantile— incapable of coherent thought, speech, or action.

This is by no means obvious to us in this life, but there are a few clues. Think of anything you might normally regard as one of your own ideas or opinions, and try to trace it to its source. We very soon find ourselves turning to a whole world of parents and teachers and friends, of books we have read and places we have seen, of experiences we have had. Or if we look in the other direction, inward, we find that "it just occurred to us," and that we have no idea where it occurred to us from. The more closely we look, the more impossible it is to say just what part of any thought, any concept, any opinion is really "ours," and what part we have received from sources known and unknown.

I am not the same person I would have been had I continued in parish ministry in 1973 instead of going into teaching. I am not the same person I would have been had I associated with different people along the way, if I had married someone else, if I had shared in the raising of different children with different gifts and different problems.

This does not mean I would be totally different, for that would be to deny the reality and the distinctiveness of the flow of life from within. What it does mean is that I cannot really tell where I leave off and the rest of the world begins. Especially in the realm of my thoughts and feelings, I cannot sort out what is "really mine" and what is others' in me.

We need to add to this the well-known fact that there are depths of our being of which we are quite unconscious. Actually, if we reflect on what happens as we move through a particular day or a particular week, we find that our consciousness of ourselves changes. One of the most familiar and useful characteristics of us as humans is our ability to "look at ourselves" without a mirror—that is, to stand back mentally and observe what we are thinking or doing, as though the person we were observing were someone else. We seem to contract our boundaries, so that part of us is outside for a while. Then there are the times when we become so absorbed in what we are doing or thinking that we are totally unselfconscious, as though there were no boundaries at all.

The image this suggests to me may sound a bit bizarre at first, but there is a good deal in Swedenborgian theology to support it. It is that we do not really change at all, from the beginning of our lives to eternity. Rather, we become acquainted with different facets and different levels of our God-given natures, and decide for ourselves which part we want to live in for eternity. There is far more to us than we can be at any one time. What we call "ourselves" is not what we actually are, but what we seem to ourselves to be; and that is ultimately determined by what we want ourselves to be. In the concise vocabulary of traditional Swedenborgianism, "we" are appearances.

Before I go on, let me cite three things from Swedenborgian theology that would seem to point clearly in this direction. The most obvious is that proprium—what we claim as ours, what we think and feel is ours—is only an appearance. The second is that for even the highest angels, their evils are not destroyed, but only "removed to the circumference." The third is that for even the worst of devils, the angelic levels of being are not destroyed, but only "closed off."

If we are appearances, then my "freedom" is as real as "I" am—which may not be very real at all. I cannot change what the Lord created. I cannot stop being the inner angel. I cannot change what I have received indirectly from ancestors and from training. I cannot abolish the evils which are such a prominent feature of my "natural." I still am the person who was born in 1931, and always will be. But as already mentioned, there is far more to that person than I can identify with. I experience that person a little bit at a time and tend to claim and cling to the aspects that I like best.

Another image from Swedenborgian theology may help at this point. Swedenborg compares the human individual to a house with several stories. All the stories must be there at birth. What we call "I" does not build that house, but lives in it. There is a delightful little parable somewhere in the writings about the pious hypocrite who sits in his parlor talking with his friends about lofty religious sentiments, and every once in a while dashes down into the cellar to have sex with his mistress. In this image, since we can't live in the whole house all at once, we find ourselves spending more and more time in the part we are most comfortable in. We have no power whatever to add or subtract stories or rooms.

Sometimes when we reflect on past events, and especially on past choices, we become oddly aware of a kind of inevitability about it all. At the time, we felt ourselves to be free agents, in control of our destiny. Looking back, we realize how strongly we were influenced by forces of which we were then unaware, and wind up wondering whether we really could have chosen other than we did. There was a time, for example, when I felt totally out of place in Convention's* ministry. I was granted the grace to express this feeling, and the response from other ministers was un-

---

* Convention refers to the General Convention of Swedenborgian Churches, the name of the Swedenborgian denomination in North America.

expectedly understanding and supportive. I chose to hang in there, and things did get better—eventually much better.

In retrospect, I cannot help wondering whether I was capable of leaving the ministry or of leaving Convention. I cannot imagine where I would have turned or what I would have done for a living. It seems now as though the critical "choice" I made was to voice my distress, and at the time that did not seem like a choice at all. It just "came out," almost against my will. It was pivotal because it was authentic and because it elicited an authentic response. It was not so much a change in me as the expression of an aspect of me that I had kept concealed, to some extent even from myself.

This is the general context in which I think I should understand those times when I know that I am on my own. In other connections, I have referred to "my military mind" or "my Pentagon"—that part of me which must be called on when there is a critical need for me to give myself orders and obey them without question. "George, you can't put this off any longer. Do it." At such times, I am operating in that realm of unreality where I seem to be an independent being. To put it in a kind of ratio, I seem to be independent, but I am not. To the same extent, I seem to be free, but I am not. Since I am for the time being confined to this level of unreality or appearance, everything balances out. My freedom is just as real as I am, and could hardly be more so.

The reality is most concisely expressed in paragraph 14 of *Soul-Body Interaction*. "God alone acts. We only react, and seen more deeply even this is from God." The mystics would agree without question. As the process of regeneration proceeds, Swedenborgian theology tells us, deeper levels of our being are opened. We have times when it goes without saying that we can accomplish something as long as we do not succumb to the illusion that we are the ones who are doing it. We learn from experience that as soon as we see ourselves as the initiators, we feel a power loss.

Taoism sees this in a way that particularly appeals to me. There is a Taoist story about a butcher who was renowned for his skill. His knives always seemed to be sharp as razors, to cut without effort. When he was asked how he did this, he answered that he never cut the meat itself. He always slipped the knife into the little spaces that were already there. He felt the places where there was no resistance.

In more general terms, he did not see himself as making anything happen. He saw himself as cooperating with the essential nature of the reality he was dealing with. The Taoist martial art, Aikido, focuses not on lethal blows, but on using the momentum of the opponent constructively. There is another story to illustrate this. A young man was on a trolley when a drunken laborer climbed aboard, shoved people out of the way, and started to batter one person who resisted. The young man watched to see how his master would use his superlative physical skills. The master went up to the drunk and said, "Something very painful must have happened to you today." The drunk collapsed in tears. The Taoist swimmer would search out ways to cooperate with the current rather that trying to master it. The whole effort is to discern the underlying pattern of things and be a constructive part of it—a profoundly ecological perspective.

I like this from a theological point of view because it helps refocus my attention especially in times of difficulty.

We sometimes betray our misunderstanding by referring to such times as "demanding." What the grace aspect of Swedenborgian theology is telling us is that the Lord is at work in this situation. It is not up to us to "fix it." What we need to do is to discern the Lord's intent and cooperate with it. This, so to speak, brings us into the current of the Lord's power, or to use a more familiar phrase, into the stream of the Lord's providence. It is a little like sailing—we do not make the boat go, we simply align it with the force that does make it go. We can blow on the sails all we want; it won't get us anywhere.

According to the many descriptions, the deepest mystical experiences go beyond this. They go to a consciousness of utter oneness. This is not so much a loss of identity as an identification with all that is, and it carries with it an effortless conviction. In one sense, the mystic in this state feels totally free, free of all limitation. But at the same time, the whole being is given into the hands of God.

In Swedenborgian terms, this must be an approach to that "inmost," to the center of our being where the Lord flows in, and at this point I must revert to the wave model again. Repetition is a hallowed teaching device, so if some of you have heard this before, it may be just as well. Or if you wish, you can simply say that I am following the example of my favorite theologian.

In physics, there is a paradoxical relationship between wave and particle models most familiar from the study of light. I would suggest that we need the same models, in the same paradoxical relationship, to understand ourselves. The particle model is the most familiar—I am what is enclosed within this skin, and am totally discrete from you.

This is useful for defining my responsibilities, but perilous for defining my rights. The more I extend my rights, the more I diminish yours.

I have already described the wave model in talking about ourselves as constituted by the intersection of direct and indirect influx from the Lord, and have mentioned that in this model, our boundaries shift. What I did not mention was that in spite of these shifting boundaries, we have a wholly constant and utterly secure identity, namely our center. That center is the essence of our being, the "place" at which we are most real. As we move out from that center, we come into realms of increasingly unreal appearances until we reach the level of "proprium"—which Swedenborgian theology tells us is an illusion.

This means that the more fully I experience my own reality, the more I realize that I am a distinctive flow of life from the Lord. My independent identity and my utter dependence are one and the same. Utter dependence is what "I" am. Swedenborg says this in language more familiar to us in *Divine Providence* n. 42—"The more the angels recognize that they are the Lord's, the more fully they seem to be themselves, and the clearer it is to them that they are the Lord's."

I know that different people have different ideas as to what is "practical." In fact, I am sometimes bemused at the fact that in theological education, "Practical Theology" deals with such issues as church administration, stewardship, and church growth. Perhaps some day, "practical theology" will be the theology that leads most directly toward heaven.

Be that as it may, I would hope that what I have said leaves you with a sense of the exquisite relationship between those times when we are gifted with grace and those times when everything is up to us. I would hope that it helps prevent us from imposing our solutions on others and inclines us rather to try to understand where they are in their process, what their present spiritual needs are. If there is one simple maxim to sum it all up, it would be that we are our best selves when we perceive what the Lord is doing and give ourselves freely to that work.

Sooner or Later

All around us, we see evidences of short-sightedness. On the personal level, we see impatient drivers snarling traffic, food stamps used for snacks rather than for nutrition, credit cards flourishing and savings accounts dwindling. On a larger scale, we see the long-range planning of Japanese industry paying dividends while our own emphasis on quick profits drains our resources. One observer has noted that television dramas create the impression that all problems can be solved in an hour, even leaving time for commercial breaks.

Perhaps the saddest thing is that this is what is commonly known as "the real world." I'm sure you've heard some variation of it— "Religious people don't face what it's like out there in the real world." The problem with this view is that deeper realities keep breaking through and showing how superficial this so-called "realism" is. There is more poverty and hunger, more crime, more failure in business, more deficit spending.

That is a glimpse of the dark side of our times, and there are countless stories to illustrate it. It is not the only side. The pressures of reality are still there, and still effective. We are beginning to face what this quick-profit and easy-living mentality is doing to our environment, to realize that disposable products save money now because they pass the costs on to our children. There is more and more attention to the roots of violence in the home, to the harm done by religious intolerance. Books that ask serious questions, like those of M. Scott Peck, make the best-seller lists.

How do we balance these two sides of the picture? Are things getting worse, or are they getting better? Is a realist an optimist or a pessimist? I believe Swedenborgian theology offers a most helpful frame of reference.

The basic notion is quite simple. The dark side that seems so evident is nothing new. It has been there all along. Now it is surfacing, and this is an opportunity as well as a threat. To take a simple example, exploitation of the environment is nothing new. There is ground in Massachusetts that still bears the scars of leather tanning operations from colonial times, and there are sites saturated with toxic chemicals from fifty and a hundred years ago. Then it happened on small enough scales that it could easily be ignored. Now, we can pollute so much more effectively that we are being forced to face the issue squarely. We should not romanticize the past. If we would look clearly at such things as the blatant corruption of the first Continental Congress, the ruthlessness of expansionism, the callous disregard of the needs of people like miners or blacks, we might find ourselves feeling grateful that we can no longer sweep such evils under the rug.

This is one thought that Swedenborgian theology brings to bear on our present situation, the thought that under the Lord's providence, latent evils are coming to the surface where they can be dealt with. Another thought is perhaps a little more elusive, but equally pertinent. It starts with the simple insistence that God is in fact good, and extends to the conviction that reality is on our side.

How does this work? It is perhaps clearest in the world of nature. This is a marvelously rich and fertile planet. There is a sense in which it is perfectly suited to us, and we to it. It is not just a collection of matter, but includes what we have long called "the laws of nature," and which we now tend to refer to as "ecological laws." We may be able to disregard them, but we cannot break them. Our actions will have consequences.

Swedenborgian theology says that these are good laws, laws designed for our well-being and happiness. This means that nature itself, so to speak, exerts an immense and constant pressure on us to take better care of ourselves. It means that we cannot go on and on doing stupid things and never finding out how stupid they are. Eventually, reality will speak, and its voice will be loud and clear. Radical as the thought may be, it can be a good thing to be faced with the realization that if we do not learn to value and care for each other, we can destroy our entire planet. We can no longer pretend that hatred and intolerance don't matter, or that they are somehow noble if our cause is just.

All this is prompted in part by recent reading about a Parliament of World Religions that was held in Chicago in 1893, and involvement in planning for a centennial parliament in 1993. There have been two recent doctoral theses on the 1893 event. One notes the failure of efforts to follow up in any formal way. There were hopes of founding a kind

17

of ongoing parliament of world faiths, and there were articles about "the next parliament," but nothing happened.

The other, more profoundly, notes that a real change occurred. Americans discovered that Hindu and Buddhist leaders were not benighted heathen, that they were beautiful and thoughtful individuals. The thought that American technology and Protestant Christianity were destined to conquer the world was shaken. The mentality that had demeaned the spirituality of American Indians was challenged. Overseas missionaries complained that their audiences were becoming more challenging, and that they were at a disadvantage if they did not understand the religion of the people they were trying to convert.

This was a real, subtle, and long-term effect. It can be traced not to any particular act, or set of acts, but to the integrity of the 1893 Parliament. The individual who conceived it, a Swedenborgian lawyer named Charles Bonney, insisted that the goal was mutual understanding, and that the focus should be on presenting the depth and beauty of one's own faith rather than on attacking others. He explicitly and wisely rejected the notion of aiming for some kind of unanimity, of coming out with "a statement" or a proposal or a program. He was also, incidentally, perfectly content to yield the limelight to others, and it is only now that his contribution is being recognized.

With some exceptions—mostly "hard-line Christians"—the speakers rose to the occasion. The Parliament called forth their best. They focused not on the external practices but on the fundamental values which those practices were designed to nurture. Rather than trying to prove that their religion was the best, they tried to present the best of their religion. Rather than trying to claim universality, they tried to touch the universal.

This strikes me as adding a valuable dimension to our thoughts about short-sightedness. Charles Bonney did not foresee what the results of the Parliament would be. He was among those who hoped and worked for a more visible continuation, so in one sense, it would seem that he was no more far-sighted than most. The major benefits of the Parliament issued from his conviction that the Divine is present in all religions and from his insistence on focusing on the best.

Similarly, we cannot see into the future, but the 1893 Parliament suggests that we do not need to. We simply need to see more deeply into the present, because the seeds of the future are here. It is in the depths of the present that we face basic issues of honesty and integrity, care and compassion, responsiveness and responsibility.

On the surface, success is everything. That is at the heart of the game that is referred to as "the real world." First you figure out what you want, and then you figure out what you have to do to get it. But things keep going wrong because that is not the way "the real world" works.

The real world of Swedenborgian theology sees things differently. First you figure out what you have to give, and then you figure out what you need in order to give it. Each of us has unique gifts, unique potential. Each of us can do some part of what needs to be done. None of us can do it all, and as technology progresses, our need of others to do the things we cannot do becomes more and more pervasive. There is no way we can be trustworthy if we overestimate our capabilities. Arrogance inevitably destroys integrity.

19

This, I would suggest, is where religion becomes a necessity for survival. Unless we believe that the Lord is perfectly loving and wise, it is difficult and perhaps even foolish to trust that integrity and compassion can be effective. On the surface, life is often capricious and unjust. We have a profound need to be in touch with depths where life is indeed fair, where laws of spirit work like the laws of nature, pressing us to care for each other.

As we discover those depths, life changes. We are more and more at peace within ourselves. We are less disoriented by unexpected turns of fortune. In one sense, we are less "worldly," but this does not mean that we are less effective. On the contrary, we can cope with difficulties far better if we can see them in proportion. When success goes to our heads, or when failure bowls us over, we can do strange and even tragic things. A trust in the underlying goodness of the Lord, in the underlying fairness of life, enables us to do what we need to do, to react thoughtfully rather than overreacting.

"Rest in the Lord, and wait patiently for him." [Psalm 37:7] This is not looking at life through rose-colored glasses. It is not some kind of unrealistic romanticism, some shallow assumption that everything will somehow turn out all right. It is the belief that whatever the appearance, reality is constructive, that the laws of nature and of spirit are firm and fair, and that living by those laws is both absolutely necessary and deeply rewarding. "The Lord is good to all, and his tender mercies are over all his works."

Deep Calls to Deep

*Deep calls unto deep at the noise of
your waterspouts: all your waves
and your billows are gone over me.
The Lord will command his
lovingkindness in the daytime, and
in the night his song shall be with
me, and my prayer unto the God
of my life.*

Psalm 42:7–8

Every once in a while, something happens that makes us suddenly aware that there are depths beneath us. We are busy with another person on some task, and that individual makes a remark that shows more feeling or sensitivity than we would have expected. We are alone, trying to sort out a routine problem, and realize that it is strangely important to us. We look in a mirror and find ourselves wondering just who it is that is looking back at us. Or at times we are simply bewildered when things that do not make sense to us seem clear to others. There is more going on than we knew, there is more to life than we had assumed.

Swedenborgian theology is primarily about those depths. It was written in the eighteenth century, and there have been a great many outward changes since then. It cannot tell us how much television the kids should watch, which foods are best for us, which candidates to vote for, or what route home we should take at rush hour. If we look at the various decisions we have to make in the course of an average day, we find that we are largely left to figure them out for ourselves.

But if we look a little deeper, we find a great deal in this theology about how to figure things out. We find ourselves enjoined to think clearly and charitably, for example. We find ourselves taught to look honestly at our own motives. We find ourselves called to think not in terms simply of profit and loss, but in terms of heaven and hell—to be mindful of our own eternal welfare and the eternal welfare of others.

This last call can sound forbidding. Sometimes people who are not feeling well do not want to go to a doctor because they are afraid they will discover that something is seriously wrong. Even more often, we may not want to look too closely at our own motives, to ask whether we are headed for heaven or hell, because we are afraid of the answer. We have looked inside enough to know that there are some things there we would rather not know.

This is exactly where Swedenborgian theology can come to our rescue, if we let it. We are all designed for heaven, and if we could see deeply enough, we would discover that heavenly design. True, it is covered over with much that is not heavenly, but that is just the covering. The simple fact that we are alive means that the Lord is flowing into us, and the Lord is perfect love and wisdom united. What we actually long for most deeply is heaven.

The covering is a real problem, though. This deepest longing comes out in some very strange forms. We long for the security of heaven and try to find it in a bigger bank account. We long for the intimacy of heaven and try to find it in sex. We long for the peace of heaven and try to find it in medications. All this is because we live so much on the surface of life and hesitate to face what lies beneath.

This is not just a private, personal problem. It is very much a problem in our relationships with each other. As I write, there is the probability that a major newspaper in New York will go out of business, one of the main issues being labor costs. There is every likelihood that neither labor nor management will give, and that both will wind up poorer. I have no idea precisely where economic justice lies in this instance, but it seems obvious that both sides are following self-defeating courses.

Let us assume that each side sees its demands as legitimate, which is usually the case. Outwardly, they cannot both be right, though they can both be wrong. Obviously, too, their demands are mutually exclusive—if one side gets more, the other side will have less. On this level, there is no hope for agreement except by compromise.

But when we look to the deeper levels, we find that the demands of both sides are legitimate and that they are not mutually exclusive. Both sides are looking for a sense of security in a very uncertain world, and there is nothing whatever wrong with that. Genuine security is a heavenly state, a state in which we can trust without reservation. By the same token, the security of one person does not threaten the security of any other. Quite the opposite, our own security is threatened by other people's insecurity, and we threaten others only when we ourselves do not feel safe.

The problem between the opposing sides, then, turns out to lie not in their ultimate goals but in the means they see as essential to those goals. I suspect, in fact, that each side feels that its demands are legitimate because the ultimate goals are legitimate. Neither side recognized the legitimacy of the other's goals because each is so exclusively focused on the illegitimacy of the demands. They are trapped at the level of competition for limited resources, and both are likely to wind up as losers as a result.

Clearly, there is not much we can do about this particular instance. However, the same thing is happening when we are at odds with each other. When other drivers are rude, the roots of this are in their longing to be where they want to be. When a teenager is rebellious, the roots of this are in a wholly legitimate longing for independence.

We may not be able to talk to the other drivers, but we can talk to the teenagers. When we do, we will have a hard time getting through unless we recognize their own sense of legitimacy, and it is hard to pretend to do this. In other words, our best chance of getting through is to look deep enough to discover what the legitimate roots of their behavior actually are. This can be particularly difficult for people who have forgotten what things felt like and looked like to them at that age.

If we do manage to get in touch with their legitimate goals, then we find ourselves allies. We recognize that something worth achieving is involved and try to help figure out appropriate ways to get there. We are no longer primarily focused on trying to prevent something we do not like, but to accomplish something we do like. Our own attitude shifts from the negative to the affirmative, and that can make a tremendous difference in itself.

I doubt that this is what the Psalmist had in mind when he wrote, "deep calls unto deep," but Swedenborgian theology suggests that this was part of the divine intent in the statement. Our depths do call out to the depths of others, tending to bring us together. All the separations, all the rivalries, all the hostilities, are much nearer the surface. It is on the surface that there may not be enough to go around. If you give someone a dollar, you have one dollar less. At a deeper level, if you give someone encouragement, you are not diminished at all. If you give someone an idea, it does not leave your store of ideas.

To me, one of the major values of Swedenborg's *Heaven and Hell* is its portrayal of what life ought to be like. His heaven is a wonderfully sane place, where people understand and care about each other. It is a wonderfully secure place, because there is no pretense or deception. People not only say what they mean, they are what they mean. The depths are uncovered. "There is nothing covered, that shall not be revealed; and hid, that shall not be known." Superficialities divide us—sometimes such superficialities as race or gender or age or education or income. The depths unite us as we begin to discover the beauty of the humanity for which we have been created.

This brings me to the final point. I mentioned earlier that we may be afraid to look inside. We have had our glimpses, and have not liked what we saw. There are those aspects of our being which we would like to keep hidden, even from ourselves. So it may actually help to remember that our Creator sees all this with perfect clarity. The Lord has searched us and known us, knows our thoughts, knows every word on our tongue. If we think that the darkness of our own deliberate ignorance will hide us, even that darkness is clear daylight to the Lord's sight.

This might sound threatening, but it should not. For the same Lord who sees us with such clarity—"in all our slobhood," as my late colleague Cal Turley would say—also treasures us with a constant love. Our fear is that if people knew what we were really like inside, they would shun us like the plague. In fact, only the Lord knows what we are really like inside. Even we do not know that ourselves. But the Lord does, and loves us.

The Lord does not love evil in any form, but can and does love us because of our profound longing for heaven. That is the whole focus of the divine attention, and the whole divine effort is toward keeping the way to heaven open for us. The Lord's attitude toward us is absolutely affirmative.

Further, the Lord is the fullest depth of all reality, and calls most directly to our own depths. There is a story in the New Testament when Nathanael realized that Jesus knew what was in his heart that he found himself called. When we are preoccupied with external events, it can be very hard to recognize what the divine will for us is. As we begin to discover our own deeper needs and longings, though, that will becomes clearer. It is the will for the kind of giving of self that draws us together in community. It is the will for a spontaneous care for each other that enables us to rest secure in each others' presence. It is the longing for heaven, which is the same thing as a longing to be an angel.

It would be idle to pretend that if we only recognize the angel in those we meet, everything will clear up in a moment. It is *not* idle to believe that if we try to do this, things will start going better. We will have more moments of mutual understanding. It will be a little easier to resolve conflicts. And if we persist over the years, our own confidence and trust will grow. We will become increasingly secure in an affirmative attitude toward each other—the attitude we would like others to have, and which we know the Lord has, toward us.

Spiritual Chaology

Understandably, I often hear people express anxiety about the direction in which our world is heading, and I suspect that I am not alone. There are times when I feel like a lonely optimist, but when I look a little deeper, I think this is an oversimplification. I'm an optimist only in regard to the future. Get me talking about the past, and I'm a pessimist.

I want to spend a little time discussing this in regard to the state of our society in general, and then give the larger part of this talk to ways in which this relates to our own individual processes of regeneration. The whole thing will be a kind of commentary on *Arcana Coelestia* n. 842 (3):

> Before anything is brought back into order, it is quite normal for it to be brought first into a kind of confusion, a virtual chaos. In this way, things that fit together badly are severed from each other; and when they have been severed, then the Lord arranges them in order.

Some of you may have seen my article entitled "The

---

* *The Messenger* is a monthly magazine published by the Swedenborgian Church.

Good Old Days" in *The Messenger** recently. It represents one specific application of an attitude toward history that I find necessary as soon as we start to look beneath the surface. Until we do, we seem to have a tendency to romanticize the past: "There were giants on the earth in those days."

Focusing on our own country, where do we look for "the good old days," when high moral standards were taken for granted? When was the solid era before the permissiveness which is often lamented? Well, things really started to fall apart in the sixties, with the hippie culture. But the fifties were the rock and roll era—surely not the golden age. The forties saw World War II, which was hardly idyllic. The thirties included the depression years, and I doubt that we would want to turn the clock back to that time. This brings us to the roaring twenties, with prohibition and speakeasies—almost a symbol of decadence. They were preceded by the decade of the First World War.

It was in the first decade of this century that child labor reached its peak. To quote the *Encyclopedia Britannica*, "In 1832, two-fifths of the factory workers in New England had been children; and by 1870 the census had reported that 750,000 children between ten and fifteen years of age were working throughout the country. Their number increased steadily from 1870 to 1910."

We might reflect on what this says about family values. These weren't high school kids working at MacDonald's after school. There was a turn-of-the-century photograph in *The New York Times Magazine* last winter. It was a picture of a miner, a grimy figure complete with hard hat, pick, and briar pipe. He looked to be about seven or eight years old.

So now we're back to the eighteen nineties; and here, because of an interest in the 1893 Parliament of World Religions, I have been doing some reading lately. Surely this was the time when solid Victorian morality reached its zenith. Well, the guiding genius of the Parliament was Charles Bonney, a Swedenborgian lawyer from Chicago. As noted above he felt that the golden age was just around the corner, and that the world—and especially America—had made tremendous progress on all fronts, including the religious.

As a lawyer, he was working diligently to clear up a few problems. He thought that juries should not be appointed on the basis of political patronage. He thought that we ought to start educational programs for immigrant laborers and work them less than eighty hours a week. He thought that saloons should be regulated in order to address the problem of widespread teenage drunkenness. If we look at the Parliament itself, we find accepted as a matter of course assumptions of white American superiority which are profoundly embarrassing. And it went without saying that the serious affairs of politics and economics needed to be in male hands.

We have twenty-twenty hindsight, if we want to use it. We can look at the eighteen-nineties and see the seeds of the troubles of the twentieth century. I would suggest that the optimism represented in the 1893 Parliament rested firmly on a remarkable ignorance of the depths of human self-centeredness, and that in good Swedenborgian terms, what we have been seeing and still see is not the breakdown of old values but the surfacing of evils that have been there all along.

"Before anything is brought back into order, it is quite normal for it to be brought first into a kind of confusion, a virtual chaos. In this way, things that fit together badly are severed from each other; and when they have been severed, then the Lord arranges them in order."

The morality of the Victorian era was all bound up with assumptions of superiority. These things "fit badly together." When they are severed, one prop, one crutch of morality, is removed, and the result is confusion. The confusion gives us a chance to rearrange things, to find better reasons for morality.

All the evidence says that we will not do this as long as we are comfortable. We have an astounding capacity to ignore anything that does not directly affect us. We may wonder at Bonney's optimism, knowing what we know, and I may criticize him for not recognizing the deep roots of the problems he identified, but he remains an admirable figure. There were not many people in the comfortable classes who took such initiatives for reform. As a man of his own times, not ours, he was pointing toward steps that could be taken then, steps that in fact were taken.

I could obviously develop this in far greater detail, but our focus is not societal so much as personal. We are far closer to that focus than it may seem. I think the point can be made by asking how many of you, if you really reflect on the issues you have faced and the difficulties you have had to deal with, would like to turn the clock back. Or I might ask how many of you feel that you used to be better people than you are now. I suspect that every one of us can look back on particular incidents and be embarrassed at characteristics we can see with such painful clarity that we wonder how we could have failed to see them at the time.

"Evil," according to *Divine Providence* n. 183 (2), "could not be taken away from anyone unless it appeared" (cf. also *Divine Providence* n. 278). It is axiomatic with us that one of the signs of progress in the process of regeneration is that we find ourselves facing deeper evils. I recall talking with an elderly lady some years ago, one of those people we would hold up as examples of the beauties of old age. She had just discovered that she really didn't like people very much.

That feeling is part of every one of us. My mind goes back to my "first term" as president of our church camp in Maine, when I was doing the opening and closing of the facilities here. I would really enjoy myself getting tents up, getting the waterfront ready, and especially battling the old galvanized plumbing. I had a personal affection for the marvelous variety of toilet tank mechanisms. The one in the Murdoch cabin especially is a work of art; it ought to be part of a guided tour of the premises, and if it is ever replaced, I want it. But as opening Saturday drew near, I would begin feeling tense. People are much harder to deal with than plumbing. You can't take a wrench to personal problems. There are very few times when you can say, "Well, that's fixed." There would be a sense of relief when everybody had left, and I was faced with straightforward tasks that allowed me to enjoy a sense of competence.

That, I would suggest, is the "normal" way of describing my attitude, of putting it in the most understandable, the least distasteful, light. What it overlooks is that galvanized pipes can't give you a smile or a hug. Even the Murdoch toilet can't ask a question or make a comment that gives a fresh glimpse of life. What it overlooks, that is, is the fact that if I had appreciated and liked people as much as I assumed I did, there would have been a mounting sense of anticipation as that Saturday drew nearer. There would have been affirmative images coming spontaneously to mind, images of those dear folk who were packing their bags and arranging to have their mail forwarded. Of course there are more strenuous responsibilities involved in dealing with people than there are in dealing with plumbing. There are also far deeper rewards.

As a number of you know, there came a time when my particular style of leadership became inappropriate. That was one of those inescapable facts that was not at all easy to accept. I don't want to make this talk into an autobiography of that particular passage of my life; but as I return to talking in more general terms, I would like you to be aware that this situation was characteristic of the way things were going for me overall, including life at home and work for the church. I was discovering myself to be "inappropriate" in a good many ways, and I was resisting the discovery.

"Before anything is brought back into order, it is quite normal for it to be brought first into a kind of confusion, a virtual chaos. In this way, things that fit together badly are severed from each other; and when they have been severed, then the Lord arranges them in order." In adolescence, we move toward a measure of independence from our parents. Previous to this, good behavior has been bound up with parental control. In the larger scheme of things, these elements "fit badly together." They have to be severed, and this brings us into a state of confusion, a virtual chaos. We are obliged to find more appropriate reasons for behaving constructively.

The reasons we find are largely egocentric, but at least they are "our own." In the early teens, we are hypersensitive to what other people think of us. From my own male point of view, I wonder whether teenage girls have any idea of their omnipotence, of how desperately boys need their acceptance and fear their rejection. There are stories I could tell . . . and I suspect that there stories all of us could tell.

There is also a tendency for things to fall apart as the process of aging becomes evident. The seeds for this are clear if we look back to the issues of adolescence. A major motivation for all our efforts has been the desire for independence, a resolve to stand on our own two feet. At our best, we want to be worthwhile members of the human community. Mixed in with this is a desire for recognition, a desire to make our mark.

This does not "fit well together" with a truly angelic life for the simple reason that we are not independent. As I stressed in another talk, our selfhood is an "appearance," in many ways an illusion. Throughout our early adult years, it is a particularly precious illusion. We matter to ourselves a great deal, and we spend a lot of time thinking about ourselves. Somewhere down inside, we are aware that we need to keep a close watch on ourselves, that we cannot afford to let ourselves get out of control.

It is not easy to let go of an illusion that is dear to us and that has helped keep us on the straight and narrow. It is scary to think that we may not be in control. We do not want to admit that we are inadequate. We like to feel good about ourselves. What this means is that we will not face the issues involved unless we become profoundly uncomfortable. Or in doctrinal terms, when these motivations are separated from the decisions involved in leading a heavenly life, the confusion seems total, and the chaos engulfing.

As some of you know, in the overall schema of the spiritual story of Scripture, I would identify this life passage with the prophets. If we think for a moment about those extraordinary books in their Biblical context, they clearly represent a major change. We move almost entirely out of the narrative mode. There is message after message, forceful and overwhelmingly negative, with little sense of connectedness or progress.

Swedenborgian theology tells us that there is a beautiful coherence and connectedness to this part of the Bible under the surface, but it does not show us that coherence and connectedness. Swedenborg draws an analogy with the process of fermentation, a process which seems entirely random, but which is actually following a very precise procedure that will result in a quite predictable chemical arrangement. One might think also of meteorology. On the scale of personal observation, it is only roughly predictable; but with the aid of satellites, we see larger patterns that begin to make sense. The more we understand the many factors involved, the more we perceive the underlying order.

But to return to the prophets, I think it is important that we recognize and accept the appearance of disconnectedness, of chaos. For now, it is enough simply to acknowledge that there must be an underlying order. In our own life processes, we really need to experience the confusion. Or to put it another way, there is a necessary correspondence of the literal disconnectedness.

I have a mild little example from my own life that might help at this point. When I chose the topic for my doctoral thesis, it was in a field where I was a relative beginner. I spent the first year amassing piles and piles of information, without any clear sense of direction. I learned a good deal about the vocabulary and syntax of the texts I was working with, but I had no idea what I was going to do with it all.

When the summer came, I filled a briefcase with notes and headed for Maine knowing that I had to sort through all this to see how everything fitted together. When I got back to Harvard in the fall, I wiped the dust off the briefcase with a dismaying sense of guilt, opened it, and took out a folder of notes. I opened it, looked at the first page in it, and knew exactly where it belonged. That second year was a very productive one, and brought the thesis into a clearly defined, well organized, and well documented state.

The simplest way to explain what happened during that first summer was that my subconscious mind found the order that was actually there, under the surface confusion. I suspect that it was a much more valid order than any that I might have worked out consciously, that my conscious mind would have been more likely to impose the order I preferred than to discover the order that was there. There was a real risk of being misled by superficial similarities, of putting things together that did not belong together, and then becoming unwilling to separate them again.

There is the same risk, I am sure, in trying to make order out of the chaotic periods of regeneration. The very reason for the chaos is that we want to hang on to inappropriate connections. If we try to follow a program, then the order we are most likely to impose is precisely the order that needs to be broken up if a better order is to ensue. We need to trust the Lord's leading more than that. We need to trust that there is a reason for the chaos, a sense that we cannot perceive.

To relate this to my previous talk, the times of chaos are times when we need to relinquish a certain measure of our control. We need to be active in regard to coping with the problems that arise, true, but we need a kind of intellectual passivity, a willingness to let the natural order of the process emerge. It is not so much an order that we can figure out with our own mental powers as it is an order that we will be able to perceive if we meet each situation as faithfully as we can. This perception will come in the Lord's good time, not necessarily—or even probably—when we think it should.

The church could be a real help at such times, and will be if we do not fall into the trap of thinking that we have to provide answers. If the order that I may try to impose on the confusion is likely to be inappropriate, if the true order is subtly working away in my spiritual depths, it would take a remarkable person indeed who could see that order from the outside in any but the most rudimentary outlines.

What is needed more than the answers themselves is the assurance that the answers are there, and that they will become clear in the Lord's good time if we persist in doing the best we can with the issues of daily life. It is helpful to be told that this is, or can be, a healthy process, that others have experienced it in their own way and have found themselves bettered by it. It is helpful to have our attention turned to what we can do about the chaos, away from the futile effort to organize it.

Perhaps it will help to be a little more specific. One of the necessary major themes of early adulthood is being in control, taking charge of our own lives. As part of this process, we learn a good deal about causes and their effects. We learn what it takes to succeed in our enterprises, what attitudes and habits are productive, and what ones get us into trouble. This creates and nourishes the illusion that we can control the future, that we can "make happen" the things we want and prevent the things we do not want.

Now Swedenborgian theology tells us that we can see the Lord's providence only after the fact. If we could see it in advance, we would interfere with it. We think we know what is best for us, and we are willing to work to attain it. If we were totally honest with ourselves, we would admit that we think we know better than the Lord does what we really need. In fact, when the sixth thing goes wrong on a particularly uncooperative day, one of the statements that is most likely to come out is, "I don't need this." Perhaps, just perhaps, the Lord is telling us that we do need it.

I can't recall anyone telling me before the fact about needing chaos and confusion. "I'm getting the feeling that I'm on the right track, and have things pretty well in hand. I think it's time I had the props knocked out from under me." I have heard people say things like this after the fact. We can look back and see what it was in us, what it was in our attitudes, that brought the crisis on.

We may not be able to see how the chaos worked. Maybe if we had kept a journal throughout the period of chaos, and then went back and analyzed it, we would be able to get a reasonably clear picture of the underlying order. That would take more time that I, for one, would be willing to spend, but it might be a task that someone else would find valuable; and if someone else did the work, I'd certainly be interested in reading the results.

I'd like to spend the rest of this talk being a little more specific about what we can do in times of chaos. I think it is best to begin by emphasizing the absolute necessity of "hanging in there" in our everyday life. Our usual motives for the faithful performance of our tasks have been badly undermined, but the tasks still have to be done. Our usual reasons for being considerate of other people have largely vanished, but we still have to go through the motions even though we don't know why. It is to be hoped that much of our constructive behavior has become habitual enough that it has a kind of momentum of its own. For example, if we have consistently resisted impulses toward physical or verbal violence, we are not likely to resort to such unfamiliar means even when things fall apart.

If we can assume, then, that we do persist in responsible outward behavior, then we may look at our deeper attitudes. I would first repeat that it helps to be reassured that there is a constructive reason for all this, that there really is a light at the end of the tunnel. Then I would suggest that we need to be asking a great many questions, and even to be asking questions about our questions. What is going on, and why? What have I done to deserve this? Why is this getting to me the way it is? Just what is it in me that feels so threatened? Why am I incapable of putting all this behind me and getting on with the business of living the way I used to? These are very general questions, which will take much more specific forms in the minds of particular individuals.

Given the willingness to ask the questions, we then

need the patience to wait for the answers. As I've implied above, the most valid answers will be gifts rather than achievements. That is, they will not be answers that we figure out by the skillful application of Swedenborgian theology. They will be insights that come to us, insights that carry conviction, that ring true.

They will have a definite relationship to Swedenborgian theology, though. While we will not find them by looking them up in the books, we will find that once they are granted, the books take on new meanings. We understand in a fresh and quite compelling way, for example, what it means to resist evils "as if of ourselves." Such familiar terms as "good" and "truth" become less abstract. Different things will jump out of the pages and seize our attention.

At first, this is likely to be an occasional experience, and more like a glimmer or a hint than a flash of light or an answer. I am reminded of the little glimpses of hope that come up from time to time in the midst of masses of prophetic denunciation. This means that we would do well to be attentive to such moments. We may not be able to prolong them, but we can at least notice and remember them so that they can be a source of encouragement.

Ultimately, if we do our part, the Lord will arrange things in a better order—a better order than the previous one, and a better order than we could devise. It is absolutely necessary that we allow the Lord to do this. That is why I have insisted that it is not our task to find answers or to impose order. Chaos is profoundly distressing; and the quickest way through it is to do our part and our part only, truly letting the Lord do what only the Lord can do.

Following the Crowd

Probably none of us would have liked Pilate's job. He was a Roman, and Judea was, against its will, a Roman province. There was an army of occupation, which did not sit well with the populace. There were tax-collectors, whom the King James Version refers to as "publicans." These were normally Jews, and they were bitterly resented as collaborators, quislings. Pilate was an administrator, charged with trying to keep the peace primarily through the use of law. There must have been many times when he weighed the consequences of possible decisions, trying to figure out what course of action would be in Rome's best interests.

As the Gospels tell it, when Jesus was brought before him, he did not find evidence of guilt. That is, he did not find evidence of conspiracy against Rome. He did find an opportunity to stand in support of the people he was governing, though. By allowing Jesus' execution, he assumed the role not of the enforcer of alien laws, but of an ally of local custom. He was on their side.

The story is so told that this is quite obvious, and that is unfortunate, in a way. Pilate's behavior is so clearly unjust that we may not identify with him. We cannot imagine "following a multitude to do evil" in such blatant fashion. We do not realize that in subtler ways, we all do. We do, simply because we are participants in a particular and very imperfect culture, and are influenced by its values in ways that are very hard to detect.

Let me give an example. As we begin to explore the solar system, there is more and more interest in searching for extra-terrestrial intelligence. Much of the time, this is accompanied by the expectation that if we do make contact, we will probably find a civilization technologically more advanced than our own. We assume, that is, that any intelligent race would share our determination to master its physical environment.

How much sense does this assumption really make? We have made tremendous strides in science and technology, in a very short time. In less than a century, we have gone from the horse and buggy to the space shuttle. Are we more contented, more at peace with ourselves, happier?

Suppose we had taken a different course. Suppose we had realized that change was needed, that we were discontented, anxious, and hostile far too often. And then suppose that we had put all our resources into probing the roots of our discontent. We would have looked to individuals who seemed to know the secrets of living peaceful and happy lives. We would have tried to understand how they got that way. We would have questioned the discontented, trying our best to understand what went wrong. We would have learned more and more about the workings of the human heart; and it would have been abundantly clear that the most genuinely successful life is characterized by generosity, compassion, and trust. There is every likelihood that we would have formed communities with far fewer material possessions, far more caring relationships, and far, far more contentment.

With this in mind, think for a moment. What are the odds that another race of humans, a more intelligent race, would have spent so much energy on things that did not deepen their happiness? Is it not far more likely that, if we do ever encounter extraterrestrial intelligence, we will find people who have learned peace?

Coming back to our text, "Thou shalt not follow a multitude to do evil," I do not mean to suggest that technology is evil, or that interest in material progress or comfort is evil. In and of themselves, they are not. The evil comes when we put them first, when we think that we will be contented if we have a new car or a new dishwasher. "If only I could win the lottery . . ." When we think like this, we turn things upside down.

When we think like this, that is, we look to be made happy by things outside ourselves. We blind ourselves to the fact that the most critical ingredient in happiness is our own attitude toward life, toward ourselves and toward others. If we were to look at the people we know who are most contented, we would find that they are not necessarily the ones who have the most. They are the people who are understanding and generous, trusting and trustworthy. Some of them may be wealthier than we, some of them have less than we.

We can make this discovery by observation, if we wish. We might be able to figure it out for ourselves. People who are generous and understanding are good to have around.

They are not out to get something from us. They are not in competition with us. They do not rouse our resentment or our competitive urges. They bring out the best in us.

If we put ourselves in the place of such people, what do we find? We find that they live in a relatively pleasing world. By and large, they are welcome wherever they go. By and large, they find people trying to treat them well. They have a kind of security that comes not from being stronger or richer, but from being valued.

This in turn rests in a very solid principle. This is a finite earth. The more of it one person or one nation monopolizes, the less there is for others. If happiness depends on possessions, then more happiness for some means less for others. But generosity is in infinite supply. It is a gift from an infinite Lord. The more one person has, the more there is for others. One person's growth in love nurtures similar growth in others. "Thou shalt love thy neighbor as thyself" is not just a lofty sentiment. It is an inexorable law of survival.

"Thou shalt not follow a multitude to do evil." "The multitude," in our own times, believes in something that is called, I hope mistakenly, "the American dream." It is the house in the suburb, with the weed-free lawn and the two cars in the garage, with the kids doing well in school and enough left over for a trip to Disneyland. It is an attractive picture, and in fact a perfectly legitimate image of contentment. Again, there is nothing wrong with it in and of itself.

Because it is attractive, and because there is nothing intrinsically wrong with it, it is awfully easy to get caught up in it. All of us, I suspect, are influenced by it to some degree. We might look at our daydreams, for example, or at that perennial question, "What would I actually do if I won the lottery?" We are part of this culture, born and raised in it. We have been taught in subtle ways that these things matter. There was an article recently that told of a man who rebelled against mowing his lawn. His neighbors were up in arms about it. His property didn't match the image.

And there, I would suggest, is the problem—it is so easy to take the image to be the essence. It's perfectly possible, of course, that the rebel was doing exactly the same thing, that not mowing his lawn was as important to him as mowing was to his neighbors. Demoting lawnmowing from the top of the list does not necessarily mean crossing it off entirely. We can recognize that outward appearances matter without believing that they matter more than anything else.

This is a good thing. It is not easy to go against the main current of one's own culture, and it helps that we are not faced with the immediate necessity of discarding something that is so widely valued. We can "keep up appearances," so to speak, but less compulsively. We can recognize that we are not proving anything about our personal worth, that we are simply doing what is expected of us. We can start to dream more about improving our relationships and less about redecorating the house.

The sooner we do, the better, because we have a long way to go. There may be nothing intrinsically evil about the house in the suburbs, but if we enlarge our vision, it is an alarming symptom. As we begin to think on a global scale and realize what abundance we have in the face of poverty and starvation elsewhere, we must realize that we are in a race with time. The world is shrinking, and we will be less and less able to ignore the effects that our choices have in other lands. More than we have realized, we are following a multitude to do evil. We are not doing it as Pilate did, face to face with the sufferer. We are not even doing it intentionally, but we are doing it none the less.

It is not easy not to do it. From time to time, there have been efforts at "redistribution of wealth," and they have not worked, Marxism being the most recent and obvious example. They have not worked, I would suggest, because they have not addressed the heart of the problem. They have assumed exactly what experience denies, that people will be contented and peaceful if they have a larger share of the world's goods. This simply is not true; and any "solution"—including capitalism—that rests upon this assumption is destined to fail.

What can we do? "Whoever is faithful in that which is least is faithful also in much." The basic shift in thinking must be away from the concept of personal ownership and toward a concept of personal stewardship. The American Indians were right. We cannot "own" the land any more than we can "own" the sky. They are ours in trust, gifts from our Creator. Whatever we have, whether it is much or little, is a resource for use. Houses and cars are not "status symbols." A house is a resource for the nurturing of family and the strengthening of friendships. A car is a means of communication, a way to enlarge the realm of our service. A television set is a means of enlarging our experience of people and places, and within limits, a perfectly valid aid to the recreation that we need.

Nor should we fall into the trap of becoming "utilitarian" in any bleak and materialistic way. We need beauty in our lives—music and art. This can certainly include pictures on the walls and curtains in the windows. The important thing is that all such beauty is to be shared rather than hoarded. We do not "own" it.

As this shift in thinking takes place within and around us, the roots of inequity will be weakened. We will find ourselves more at peace, and becoming peacemakers. We will find our nation becoming a more responsible citizen of the planet as "the multitude" tends more and more toward the good.

"Organized" Religion?

The thoughts I want to put before you started some five or so years ago when I was asked to be a consultant in developing a film on William Blake and Swedenborg. When Blake was (I think) in his late twenties, he read Swedenborg's *Divine Love and Wisdom*, and the comments he wrote on the margins of his copy indicate a sense that he had found a kindred spirit. This is probably why he attended a meeting in London where readers of Swedenborg were to take the first steps toward founding a distinct church organization. He signed the register on the first day and apparently never came back. In fact, for years thereafter, his comments on Swedenborg are largely negative; and it was only late in his life that he seemed to return to his favorable stance.

What happened? The proceedings of that first meeting were recorded, and I quote a part of the published account.

> . . . the Circular Letter, convening the Conference, was read. The Meeting then proceeded, with a solemnity and deliberation suited to the magnitude of the occasion, to take into serious consideration the various Propositions contained in the above Letter;

and after a most interesting and instructive conversation on their important contents, the following Resolutions were moved, and unanimously agreed to.

There follow thirty-two theological statements describing essentials of Swedenborgian theology in catechetical fashion and proclaiming the absolute truth of that theology, the hopeless falsity of contemporary Christianity, and the need of a "complete and total Separation" between the two.

In his own way, Blake might well have agreed that the new theology was a revelation, and that the Christian church of his day had wandered hopelessly far from the intent and spirit of the Christ. He would have disagreed totally with the solution proposed, both in style and in content. In content, the whole notion of establishing a new orthodoxy would have been repellent. He described his own calling as a calling "to open the immortal eyes of man inward, into the bosom of God." There was no way he would trade his liberty of thought for conformity to any creed. In style, his excitement and creativity were diametrically opposed to the "solemnity and deliberation" of the meeting. I cannot prove it, but I have a moral certainty that his brief exposure to this approach to Swedenborgianism occasioned his little poem, "The Garden of Love," which includes the following lines.

> I went to the Garden of Love
> And saw what I never had seen:
> A Chapel was built in the midst
> Where I used to play on the green.
> . . . .

And Priests in black Gowns
Were walking their rounds
And binding with Briers
My Joys and Desires.

The main issue I see here was not a new one at the time, and it has not gone away in our own times. It is the issue of institutionalism and religion. In her book *The Gnostic Gospels*, Elaine Pagels [New York, Random House, 1981] presents a vivid picture of the dynamics of this issue in the early history of Christianity. The Gnostic stressed the possibility and the necessity of a direct individual relationship with the divine. The institutionalist saw this as a straight road to chaos, and stressed the need for some kind of law and order.

I find it increasingly difficult to see this as simply a conflict between the good guys and the bad guys, though I identify more strongly with the gnostic approach than with the institutional. The peril of individualism is the neglect of community. Some of the gnostics were pretty flaky. But more than that, I believe that we are essentially social beings, with a fundamental and profound need to learn from each other both mentally and emotionally.

The peril of institutionalism, though, is no less real, and seems on reflection surprisingly similar. It seems in fact to be the same problem on a larger scale. It is separatism, the isolation of the institution from the larger community. The church becomes *the* church, the sole repository of truth, obliged to maintain its orthodoxy rigorously and sadly obliged to proclaim the error of all others.

If I push this line of thought a little further, I come to a consideration of matters of difference, right, and wrong. I would state first of all that I do not think it is possible to be human without notions of right and wrong. To be human is to choose, and to choose is to adopt one course of thought or action as better than another. I cannot conceive of a way of being human that does not involve values.

The problem is that we seem to have a hard time believing that there are differences that are not differences in value. It is hard to suggest that there are significant differences between the sexes or between races without becoming, or being regarded as, a sexist or a racist. It is hard to become committed to one church without becoming, or being regarded as, disapproving of others.

I hasten to add that churches are not the only institutions that fail to solve this problem. In fact, I would go so far as to suggest that, by and large, they face it more squarely and handle it much better than most secular organizations. What would happen, for example, if you went to a local football game and cheered for the opposition? What would happen if you went to work for one company and openly promoted the product of a rival? What would happen if you wrote to your local newspaper suggesting that your town was getting more than its share of state aid?

No, to me the fact of Vatican II, the fact of the ecumenical movement, and the facts of common pulpit exchanges, indicate to me that "the world," the secular world, has a long way to go to catch up with many churches. Such churches and temples seem to have found a way to recognize difference without crossing the border into rejection.

Some, obviously, have not. It seems characteristic particularly of fundamentalism, whether Christian, Muslim, or Jewish, to deny the validity of all who disagree. To me this demeans rather than exalts the divine, since it limits the effective power of the divine to one small group. *Extra ecclesia nulla salus*— there is no salvation outside the church— claims that God can heal, bless, and save only within these organizational boundaries. I would rather put it the other way around. *Extra salutem nulla ecclesia*—unless there is healing, blessing, and saving, there is no church.

Should there then be just one vast church organization, comprising all people who identify with the healing and the blessing? This is certainly not a realistic goal for our own times, but I find it suspect on deeper grounds as well. Swedenborg offers a thought that has grown on me recently, "That a form makes a one the more perfectly in proportion as the things which enter into it are distinctly different, and yet united" (*Divine Providence*, n. 4 [4]).

On an individual level, I have a peculiar contribution to make, which I cannot make effectively to the extent that I try to resemble others or to differ from them. I do not need to imitate some stereotype in order to be male. I happen to be male, one little syllable in an ongoing definition of that term. In fact, by imitating a stereotype, I distort the definition, as though the "cu" in the word "masculine" decided it didn't belong because it wasn't a "mas."

But that is not the whole picture. By itself, it would indicate that my primary obligation is simply to "do my own thing." One essential part of my own distinctiveness, though, is the unique set of relationships in which I am involved. Think for a moment of how hard it would be to maintain a particular self-image if all the feedback you got from others contradicted it. Whatever the mirror says, could you regard yourself as unattractive if everyone seemed to want you around? Could you regard yourself as attractive if everyone tried to avoid you?

That is an obvious oversimplification. We actually get mixed signals from others, and usually wind up with a good deal of latitude in deciding who we are. It seems, then, that our real "own thing" is both self-generated and conditioned. It is not an either/or situation. In fact, if we find individuals who are not responsive to conditioning or individuals who respond mechanically, we label them catatonic or obsessive-compulsive, respectively, and often despair of helping them.

Where does this leave me in regard to "organized religion?" I'm almost embarrassed by the simplicity of the conclusion, so I'll say it first in abstract terms, that the task of every church is to reconcile individuality and interdependence. Differences are "better" as they promote that reconciliation, and "worse" as they impede it, as they promote individualism at the cost of unity or unity at the cost of individuality. In more everyday language, the task of each organized church is to identify and make its own very special contribution to oneness.

A Serving Church

We face a particular dilemma as members of a Swedenborgian church. On the one hand, we are members largely because we believe that the theology of this church is more satisfactory than other theologies. On the other hand, that theology itself insists that the Lord works effectively through all religions. We are unwilling to make truth completely relative, to say only that this theology is best for us. We would really like to say that it is best for everyone. Yet time after time we are faced with the clear statement that "good people in all religions are saved," and there seems little point to a theology other than as a means to salvation.

At least part of the problem centers in the institutional nature of the church. Historically, one joins only one church at a time. Membership involves commitment, and commitment to one church is normally understood to preclude commitment to another. This in itself strikes me as simply an extension of our own individual self-concern, our tendency as individuals to try to defend our own worth by minimizing the worth of others. Children can fear that their parents' love for their siblings means that there is less love for them. Married partners can want a relationship that excludes not only infidelity but even close friendships. Husbands are traditionally often jealous of their children, and wives of their husbands' jobs.

In what Swedenborg refers to as the natural world, there is some justification for this. Physical time, space, and resources are limited. Time spent on one relationship means that there is less time for others. Money spent on one enterprise means that there is less available for others. An institutional church, then, has some reason to want its members to make a kind of exclusive commitment. It is conscious of its own needs, and it may feel threatened if its members are actively involved in another church.

In the mental and spiritual realms, however, we find what seems to be a quite different situation. Love for one child does not diminish love for another. Understanding of one individual does not mean misunderstanding others. In fact, the ability to love and understand one person enhances the ability to love and understand others. Conversely, the inability to form or sustain friendships bodes ill for a marriage relationship, just as the inability to sustain a loving marriage bodes ill for relationships with children.

I suggested that this only seems to be different from the physical situation. With the rising number of marriages in which both parents work, there has been a good deal of attention to what happens to children who do not have a parent around the house all day. The evidence consistently indicates that it is not the amount of time that parents spend with their children that counts most, but the quality of that time. The mother who is in the house all day getting cabin fever, experiencing the children as constantly demanding, is not necessarily a better mother than the one who comes home from work tired, but experiences the children as special.

Of all institutions on earth, the church is supposed to be the one that focuses on and represents spiritual values. This sometimes reaches the proportions of caricature, to be sure. There have been countless Christian groups that have taught and practiced "renunciation of the world" and have regarded money in particular as evil. But at its best, religion demonstrates that living for others works, not just inwardly, but outwardly as well. "Seek ye first the kingdom of God, and His righteousness, and all these things shall be added unto you." "Be ye therefore wise as serpents, and harmless as doves." It may not lead to wealth and power, but the Christian life wisely led, because it involves usefulness and its material rewards, does provide food and shelter. It does provide a sense of security, partly because material needs do not become obsessions.

If this is true of the religious life of the individual, we may suspect that it is true of the collective life of the institutional church. That is, the church that is primarily concerned with its own physical survival will be prey to anxiety. The church that tries to assert its own worth by demeaning the worth of others will find itself increasingly isolated and embattled. The church that demands exclusive commitment will find resentment growing in its membership. There will be fights over money and property, and struggles for power.

We as Swedenborgians have a clear alternative to this, I believe. It is implicit in the insistence of Swedenborgian theology that the Lord is at work everywhere, bringing salvation not just among our own small numbers, not just within the bounds of Christianity, but wherever people try to live by principles which they regard as coming from a source beyond themselves. I think this alternative could be developed into a style of church commitment, almost a program.

We begin with this assumption about the Lord's universal care and work, and add only the assumption that our task as a church is to cooperate with the Lord in His work. That seems fairly safe and obvious. It then follows that we can best cooperate if we find out how the Lord is offering salvation through other religions, and see whether there is anything we can do to help.

Every earthly church has its spiritual liabilities as well as its spiritual assets. Every earthly church needs help. We have some very special resources to bring. We need not expect people to "buy the whole package" of Swedenborgian theology, but we may very well have unique and helpful insights. As individuals who have tried to learn and live by these principles, we may have very special skills.

Suppose, then, that we took it as our task to help other churches, other religions, become more effective vehicles of the Lord's salvation. Suppose we took it as our task to seek out church programs to which we could contribute some time, thought, and skill. Suppose that wherever one of our churches was found, there were supportive, helpful Swedenborgian presences in various ventures of other churches, a consistent voice for the practical realization of spiritual values. What would happen to our church?

First of all, I suspect that it would find itself studying both its own theology and the theologies of other churches.

We would fail if we went out as "the people with the answers," if we set out to straighten out all those poor mistaken folk out there. We would find ourselves in complex situations, with no easy answers. We would find ourselves coming to our own church with questions. We would have a particular interest not in theology in the abstract, but in theology as the disciplined and intelligent examination of principles to live by, of ideas that affect decisions and relationships. Most importantly, we would be looking at other systems to find out what is right about them, to find out what the Lord is providing as means to salvation.

Second, I suspect that we would begin to attract people who have tended to be repelled by some of the features of institutional religion. By helping Catholics be better Catholics, Methodists to be better Methodists, Jews to be better Jews, we would recruit precisely those people who saw the validity and the value of this task. Some might not in fact leave their "religions of origin," but they would be sources of encouragement, enlightenment, and support.

Third, we would come to see ourselves, and to be seen, as really worth having around. We could look at the growth of another church with the knowledge that we had helped. We could know that other people were probably talking about our useful contributions behind our backs, that our reputation as a helpful resource was growing.

It would take time and effort. I am sure that some of it is being done. In most of our churches that I have known, there have been individuals with some involvement in projects sponsored by other churches. Nowhere, though, have I found this regarded as an explicit feature of commitment to the church. Nowhere have I found an effort to build

61

on the experience, to develop the understanding and the skills to help as effectively as possible.

The doctrinal basis for such an approach is clear. Even the apostle Paul, who is so often used to justify exclusive Christianity, wrote to the Romans about ". . . the righteous judgment of God; who will render to every man according to his deeds: . . . Glory, honour, and peace, to every man that works good, to the Jew first, and also to the Gentile: for there is no respect of persons with God" (Romans 2:5, 6, 10, 11). Isaiah foresaw a time when Israel would be a blessing between her ancient enemies, Assyria and Egypt. The Lord found a matchless faith in the presumably "pagan" Roman centurion. What might we find, if we went out and looked?

Bands of Love

I drew them with cords of a man,
with bands of love: and I was to
them as they that take off the yoke
on their jaws, and I provided
them food.

Hosea 11:4

This is an extraordinary image, especially set against the background of the events it refers to. Hosea is talking about the whole history of Israel—the call to Abram, the gifts of descendants, the time in Egypt, the deliverance, the leading through the wilderness, the conquest of the Promised Land, and the establishment of a secure nation under David. There were many ways in which the Lord guided the people in this long series of events. There were messages to particular individuals, miracles of deliverance, and severe punishments for transgression.

From a human point of view, these different means may seem totally different. We do not experience rewards and punishments in the same way, and neither did Israel. As a result, we find the Lord portrayed as changing, sometimes radically. One moment he is pleased, the next moment angry. One moment he is gentle and forgiving, the next moment rigid and demanding. But under this guise of changing means, Hosea is shown a constancy. These are all "bands of love." Through the whole process, the Lord is constantly trying to lead this chosen people to their rest, to the time when the yoke can be taken off and the food provided.

We often find a parallel drawn between this and parenting, and this works very well up to a point. The parent who loves a child wisely will say "No" on occasion, and if necessary will back the refusal up with punishment. The main problem with this comparison is that even the best parents are not always at their best, and in most discipline there is an element of self-centeredness. The child's behavior bothers the parent, and the discipline may not be primarily for the sake of the child.

I hasten to add that self-concern, as opposed to self-centeredness, is not only legitimate but necessary. The parent is not supposed to be a martyr. Ideally, what is best for the child is also best for the parent. In either case, it may require abandoning some short-term goal, and it is likely to feel like a sacrifice; but those who have seen their children grow into responsible and responsive adults know that the rewards of their efforts are deep and abiding. The yoke has been taken from their jaws as well.

Swedenborgian theology offers a most appealing way of visualizing this process. Early in *Arcana Coelestia*, Swedenborg writes as follows:

> When we are dead [meaning dead to the Lord's love and light], we almost always come out the loser in life's struggles; and when there is no

64

struggle, the dominant forces within us are evil and false, and we are slaves. Our restraints are outward ones, restraints such as fear of the law, of losing our lives, or our resources, or our profit, or the reputation such things afford us.

When we have become spiritual, we are always victorious in life's struggles. The restraints that guide us are inner ones and are called the restraints of conscience.

Once we have become heavenly, we no longer experience struggle. If evil and false forces assail us, we simply have no use for them. This is why we can be called "victors." There are no visible restraints guiding us: on the contrary, we are free. The invisible restraints are our perceptions of what is good and true. (n. 81)

We are so familiar with systems of reward and punishment that we take them quite for granted. We know about parking tickets and fines, we see police cars and radar guns. In our present involvement with the crisis over drugs, we are acutely aware that our society depends on "external restraints" for its very survival. We avoid walking city streets at night because we know that these restraints cannot be perfect, and that where they are missing, there is real and present danger.

We may become so preoccupied with this aspect of our world that we fail to notice the other. We read about the arrests for drunken and reckless driving, and let that fill our horizon. If we observe dispassionately, though, it seems that the vast majority of drivers is behaving reasonably well.

Thousands upon thousands of people signal their turns, stay in lanes, and stop at lights. In the same vein, thousands upon thousands of people are not addicts and do not resort to theft and violence. Or again, we take for granted the regular stocking of supermarket shelves, without thinking of the countless people who had to do their jobs faithfully in order for this abundance to be accessible to us.

In short, we live in a mixed world, where some need to be restrained by fears of punishment, where some have developed the restraints of conscience, and where some, if only a few, have caught a vision of goodness so appealing that callous behavior has no attraction.

The message of Swedenborgian theology is that we can progress in this regard. We all began life with a need for outward restraints. We have apparently all reached the point where I do not need to promise you cookies if you sit still through the sermon, where in fact you would think it pretty ridiculous if I did. The whole effort of the Lord's providence is to keep us in freedom, to have constantly available to us a next step in the direction of heaven. This holds true no matter how far from heaven, or how near to heaven, we may be. In *Arcana Coelestia* again, we find the statement that the judge who "punishes malefactors according to the laws . . . is in charity toward the neighbor; for he wills their amendment, and thus their good" (n. 4730). There are cases of recovery from alcoholism, and of rehabilitation from criminal behavior.

This makes it particularly damaging when punishment is regarded as an end in itself. The criminal is to be penalized simply because of the past, and not at all for the sake of the future. That may well be the way the criminal sees the situation, but that is hardly a reason for others to take the same view. A recent newspaper article told of difficulties in funding "college-in-prison" programs in spite of the fact that none of the former inmates who had gotten college degrees had had further trouble with the law.

Christianity is not blameless in this regard. It is not hard to find instances of blatant injustice in the name of religion, of course, but there is a more subtle and pervasive distortion that often goes unnoticed. Whenever hell is portrayed as a place of punishment for past sins, a climate of thought is nurtured in which punishment is regarded as an end in itself.

Here, as in many cases, Swedenborgian theology is quite explicit. First of all, the Lord never punishes anyone (*Arcana Coelestia* n. 2447). The punishment is the inevitable consequence of the evil. That is precisely why it is evil, because it hurts. In this life, we are often so absorbed in outward matters that we are insensitive to what is happening within. Time after time, people set their hearts on some goal, pursue it heedless of others, and are quite blind to the fact that they are anxious, tense, and suspicious—in fact quite unhappy. To the extent that they are aware of this, they blame it on circumstances rather than acknowledging the extent to which they are bringing it upon themselves.

This is the reason for a second point Swedenborgian theology makes about hell, which on first hearing sounds even more startling. It is that no one is punished after death for sins committed before death. There is no point to this in the spiritual world. If the person has changed, then punishment would serve no purpose. If the person has not changed, then the evil will continue, and will contain its own punishment.

To think otherwise is to believe that evil is getting caught. It is to believe that evil would make us happy if it were not for the punishment that is arbitrarily attached to it. Ultimately, it is to believe that the Lord has made some forms of behavior bad by making rules against them and imposing penalties for them, and that if it were not for those penalties, evil would be good.

This kind of belief represents a kind of getting stuck in the first kind of restraint. It assumes that we cannot develop beyond the need for restraint by fear; and it has an implication that may be surprising, namely that a pessimistic view of human nature goes hand in hand with a negative image of the Lord.

It may seem as though we can exalt the Lord by contrast, so to speak, that we can emphasize the Lord's goodness by emphasizing our own evil. It seems, instead, that all this accomplishes is a kind of lowering of the whole scale. Everything and everyone, including God, becomes more grim. As we see ourselves more and more like criminals, the world becomes more and more like a prison, and the Lord becomes more and more like the warden. But the unseen restraints of heavenly people are their perceptions of what is true and good. These are glimpses of the Lord's nature and presence. This is the beauty of the Lord beginning to be seen through the distortions of evil.

"I drew them with cords of a man, with bands of love: and I was to them as they that take off the yoke on their jaws, and I provided them food." Swedenborg says in a number of places that punishment comes from the Lord's mercy, both because it protects the innocent and because it desires amendment. I would suggest that at the deepest level, punishment stems from mercy because evil itself is unmerciful.

What is it like to feel vengeful? What is it like to want to see the malefactor suffer? It is to find delight in another's pain, and this feeling can be amplified by the presence of mercy. In essence, evil recoils from the Lord's presence, and in so doing distances itself from all genuine blessing.

As we review our lives, we can surely remember many times when things have gone wrong. It is to be hoped that in retrospect, we can see the good that has resulted and can realize that this was no accident. This was the Lord's underlying intent. These were the unseen bands of love, and they are with us now.

How Silently?

We are living in years of widespread and unexpected change. Most noticeably, the sudden collapse of the Soviet Union has shattered the polarized "us against them" situation that we had taken for granted as the most important fact about world politics. We are discovering what we could have found out long before, if we had inquired, that that "Union" included a vast diversity of peoples, with very different languages and cultures.

We have a tendency to use this as a sign of the triumph of capitalism, but our own continuing economic distress raises a warning flag. As suddenly as the Soviet Union collapsed, it seems that we recognized the greed and corruption that were the hallmark of the eighties, and realized that greed, the driving motivation of laissez-faire capitalism, was not a sure foundation for our country. We have some hard rethinking to do, and the pressure on us is growing year by year and even month by month.

What does this have to do with Christmas? Perhaps very little, which is why I have mentioned it. Two thousand years ago, there were also major events brewing. The Roman Empire was nearing its zenith. In the Holy Land, the forces were building that would lead to the destruction of the Temple in the year seventy, and an expulsion of Jews from their homeland that would last effectively until the British Mandate of 1918. In the face of all this upheaval, all these matters of empire, the birth of a child in the small town of Bethlehem would not make the back pages, let alone the headlines.

As it happened, that birth was more important than all the diplomatic moves and military campaigns of the centuries. In that infant, God was coming to earth in a way that would eventually touch the minds and hearts of millions of individuals, but at the time, hardly anyone noticed. At the close of Matthew's Gospel we find Jesus saying "All power is given to me in heaven and on earth," yet even this was said only to a chosen few.

Perhaps, then, at Christmas time we should question our own assumptions about what is important. Are we any more alert to the moving of the Lord among us than were the people of two thousand years ago? Is there, somewhere among us, a child being born, or a life being lived, that will make future generations stop and wonder? Is something stirring in our own hearts that will grow until it transforms our lives?

We do not anticipate a physical second coming. We believe that the epochal second coming happened with the opening of the spiritual meaning of Scripture through the agency of Swedenborg. But by the same token, we believe that the Lord is always standing at the door and knocking—or more appropriately for the season, that the Lord is always ready to be born in us.

Maybe it is happening to us or to someone near us.

Would we notice? It might be just a moment of unexpected compassion or insight. It might be a momentary gift of hope, an unbidden sense that even our mundane lives could be touched by beauty. It might be a realization that we are not alone, or a glimpse of goodness in another individual where we had thought there was little or none.

These are little, momentary events, but their size is not what matters. Jesus did not gain all power in heaven and on earth by gathering thousands of followers or amassing incredible wealth. He did so by the quality of his life, by overcoming the hells he met within his own spirit. In exactly the same way, the significance of "little" moments is not determined by their size but by their quality. It is the truth of the insight that matters, not its scope. It is the purity of the compassion that matters, not its apparent power or extent.

These moments are not of our making. They are gifts from the Lord. Our part is vital, though—it is to recognize and accept them when they happen. If we could review our lives in detail, we might be profoundly depressed to discover how many times we have been offered the lovely impulse or the clarifying insight and have ignored it. We have been too preoccupied with our own agendas, too wrapped up in the things we consider important, to notice that a child was being born in us. After all, babies can't put a roof over our heads or food on the table.

Our heavenly father knows that we have need of food and clothing and shelter. There will be people dying on the city streets these cold nights, and we do not want to be among them. But if that is where our concern ends, if all we think about is our own self-preservation, then we are constraining our souls into an ever shrinking compass, into the prison of our selfishness.

What the Lord would bring to birth in us is a generous motion, a reaching out to each other. It is what he described in the text of his first sermon in the synagogue at Nazareth— "to heal the broken-hearted, to preach deliverance to the captives, and recovering of sight to the blind, to set at liberty them that are bruised." For we are captive not to Rome or to any earthly power, but to our own fears. We are blinded not by physical disease but by our own insensitivity.

Phillips Brooks put together the words that keep calling to us, year after year: "How silently, how silently the wondrous gift is given! So God imparts to human hearts the blessings of his heaven." If we truly want those blessings— and there are times when we do not—if we trust the pattern which is disclosed in his own life among us, then we should not look for great events, for some dramatic conversion. We should look instead for the little gifts that are being offered us every day, out of the constancy of the Lord's love for us. We should pay heed to every glimmer of understanding, every little warming of our hearts. It is from such small beginnings that the kingdom of heaven can grow in us, if we have the wisdom to search for the babe, and come, and adore.

Christian Theology
and
the Holographic Model

Part I
Basic Principles

M y Random House dictionary defines theology as "the field of study, thought, and analysis that treats of God, His attributes, and His relations to the universe; the science or study of divine things or religious truth." By this definition, the Gospels do not present "a theology" or a Jesus who was "a theologian," at least not a systematic one. I suspect this is why Protestant Christianity has made such extensive use of Paul's letters. They at least seem to present a theology.

The Jesus of the Gospels used parables, questions, and paradoxes extensively. While he may have "explained everything to his disciples" in private, little of that explanation is available to us; and we are left much more in the position of the crowds who were obliged to find their own meaning—except that the church has over the centuries expended a great deal of time and energy telling us what meanings we are supposed to find.

What that meaning is depends on the church you belong to. The range of options is wide indeed. Fundamentalist, pentecostal, evangelical, unitarian, gnostic, ritualistic, activist, and idealistic versions of the Christian message are all currently available, sometimes delineated by denominational labels, sometimes within a single church body.

It seems to come down to a matter of personal history and personal choice. Current events have highlighted similarities between the fundamentalist Islam of Khomeini and fundamentalist Christianity, suggesting that in Islam as well as in Christianity there is enough ambiguity to nurture different interpretations by different personality types, or to meet different needs. We have tried very hard, but Jesus' teaching method is still at work. There is a fundamental ambiguity that requires us to find our own meaning.

It has come as a surprise to me to discover this ambiguity in my own Swedenborgian tradition. Swedenborg was, after all, a theologian, with a high respect for God's gift of rationality. He wrote copiously and quite explicitly. I was alerted to the ambiguity especially by the realization that William Blake attended the first session of the first General Conference of Swedenborgians in London in 1789, and that his hostile attitude toward Swedenborg began about that time.*

---

* See p. 51, "Organized Religion?," for a more complete account of Blake and that first historic meeting of Swedenborg readers.

It is fertile ground for imagination. Blake had read Swedenborg's *Divine Love and Wisdom* and had reacted with passionate enthusiasm. He then attended a meeting where thirty-two theological propositions—none drawn from *Divine Love and Wisdom*—were proposed, discussed, and unanimously adopted as justifying the founding of a separate church organization. In a sense, Blake must have seen his own "liberation theology" dogmatized, and dogmatized in the very words of the theologian he had seen as the liberator.

While this image was engaging my attention, I was also becoming acquainted with the thought of Karl Pribram and David Bohm on the holographic model. It attracted me because it contained statements that reminded me of statements in *Divine Love and Wisdom*. These were statements that I had taken as presumably true in a philosophical sense, but as basically incomprehensible, statements such as "The Divine is the same in the greatest and the smallest things." (*Divine Love and Wisdom* n. 77). It struck me that the same idea was presented in quite different language by Blake—

> To see the World in a grain of Sand,
> The Universe in a Wild Flower,
> Hold Infinity in the Palm of your Hand,
> And Eternity in an Hour.

The result of all this is that I am coming to see Swedenborg's theology differently than I did before. I am coming to see it as composed of a central holographic concept entering a matrix of pietistic Lutheranism. I am eager to share this view especially while it is still plastic, since it engenders a suspicion of systems worked out by individuals in supposed isolation.

In fact, I should like the view to remain plastic. Swedenborg insists that pure, divine truth is beyond mortal or even angelic grasp, that we may only progress, to eternity, from less adequate to more adequate "appearances of truth" (*Arcana Coelestia* n. 3207 [3]). What follows is presented as a potentially productive way of viewing reality, then, and not as a literal description of it.

It is an observable fact that holograms work. They do make three-dimensional images, and any part of the holographic plate does contain the entire image. I have read, to my surprise, that by using film with microscopically fine grain, one can make a hologram of a leaf and examine the cellular structure under a microscope.* I stress this actuality because the whole matter can seem quite theoretical and unlikely.

The holographic plate is a record of the interference pattern of light waves. It is as though two pebbles were tossed into a still pond, and the surface were flash-frozen after the ripples had criss-crossed the whole surface.

The light used is coherent light from a laser so that the waves will be uniform and intelligible. The beam is split and spread, and half reflected off the object being recorded. If the developed plate is properly illuminated, it creates a three-dimensional image. I think of it, rightly or wrongly, as an incredibly intricate set of prisms, bending the light

---

* Stanislav Grof, *Beyond the Brain: Birth, Death, and Transcendence in Psychotherapy* (Albany: State University of New York Press, 1985), p. 78.

back into the patterns that occasioned them. Cut the plate into pieces, and each piece will create the whole image, though the smaller the fragment, the less detail there will be, and the more precise the angles of illumination and viewing must be.

Karl Pribram found in this a model for understanding memory functions in the human brain. As a neurosurgeon, he was well aware of the phenomenon of "distributed memory," the fact that damage to particular areas of the brain does not remove specific memory traces. As he observed, you don't get hit on the head, come home, and discover that you've forgotten half of your family. Dr. Pribram is also aware that this has metaphysical implications, that the thought of all information being simultaneously present everywhere is strongly reminiscent of some descriptions of the Divine.

This kind of modeling raises a fundamental epistemological point with special relevance for theology. Theology deals very largely with matters that cannot be weighed and measured—with salvation, grace, the soul, judgment, and the divine, for example. In keeping with Swedenborg's dictum that our apprehension is limited to "appearances," I would suggest that we normally think and communicate about these unseen matters by using images drawn from common physical experience. Jesus' use of parables would seem to validate this practice; but it should also caution us against taking our images too literally. Conceiving of redemption, for example, as Jesus' "paying the price" for our release from bondage may point to some significant aspects of the process of salvation, but if it is taken as a precise description of "what actually happens," the Gospel emphasis on fruitful lives as a means to union with the Divine tends to be lost.

Exploring the holographic model involves a whole new set of images. They are drawn from the wave properties of matter, and for this reason they foster an awareness of the fact that most of our commonly accepted images are drawn from the particle properties of matter. There is a fundamental and important difference. Two particles cannot occupy the same space at the same time. Waves superimpose on each other without losing their distinguishable identities. A single groove on a record can represent a full orchestra and the Mormon Tabernacle Choir singing the "Hallelujah Chorus," and within the limits of technology, the listener can still pick out the tenor line or the second violins.

When we talk about our own inner processes or our relationships with each other, we often use images that are strikingly Newtonian, if we take note of them. They rest, that is, in particle characteristics of matter. We talk in terms of stress, friction, tension, leverage, balance, pressure, action and reaction, breaking points, and drive, for example. We do so, I would insist, because these are useful images. I would not for a moment propose replacing such images with wave images in theology or psychology any more than a physicist would propose doing so in accounting for the properties of light. It seems rather that particle images need wave images as their complement, and my attention to the holographic model needs to be an effort to find a balance. In mood it is rather like trying to balance a Synoptic pragmatism with a Johannine spirituality.

I'll be coming back to questions of epistemology from

time to time, but in order to establish the connection between Swedenborg and holography, I need to set the ontological scene. Swedenborg does this fairly concisely in nos. 3627f. of *Arcana Coelestia*:

> It is a general rule that nothing can come into being and endure from itself, but only from something else—that is, through something else. It is also a general rule that nothing can be held in a form except by or through something else, as we can conclude from everything in nature. It is recognized that the human body is held together in its form from the outside by the atmospheres; so unless it were also held together from the inside by some active or living force, it would instantly collapse. . . .

> As we have just stated, there are always two forces that are holding any entity together in its integrity and in its form, namely a force acting from the outside and a force acting from the inside, with the thing that is being held together in the middle. This is true of the human being in even the smallest parts. It is acknowledged that the atmospheres are what hold the whole body together from the outside, by their constant pressure or weight, and also that the air-atmosphere does the same for the lungs through its inflow. It does the same for its own organ, the ear, with its inner forms built for the modifications of the air. . . . Unless there were corresponding inner forces that were reacting to these outer forces, holding the intermediate forms together and keeping them in balance, they would not last even a moment. We can see from this that there must at all costs be two forces if anything is

to come into being and last. The forces that flow in
and act from within are from heaven, and come
through heaven from the Lord, and they have life
within them.

I would make three observations about this passage.
One is that it does have a distinctly Newtonian cast about
it. It talks about action and reaction, and about keeping
things in a balance. This may serve to illustrate that the
wave model complements rather than replaces the particle
model.

The second observation is simply to highlight its emphasis on the image of intersecting forces, the assertion that
the "particle nature" of every discernible "thing" rests in
confluences of forces.

The third observation is that Swedenborg elsewhere
maintains that the "force from the outside" is also from the
Lord, but indirectly (cf. *Arcana Coelestia* n. 7004 [2]). In
Divine Love and Wisdom n. 5 he uses one of his favorite
images to express this, seeing the Lord as a sun whose
warmth is love and whose light is truth:

We need to realize that warmth and light eminate
from that sun, that the emanating warmth is essentially love and the emanating light essentially wisdom. . . . That sun itself (or divine love) cannot use
its heat and its light to create anyone directly from
itself. For such a creature would then be love in its
essence, which is the Lord himself. That sun can
however create [people] from substances and materials so formed that they can be receptive to essential warmth and light. It is rather like the way the

82

> physical sun cannot use its warmth and light to
> produce vegetation directly from the ground, but
> uses materials from the soil. . . .

This is an image of first creating a matrix receptive of life, and then vivifying it—of first creating the dust of the earth, if you will, and then breathing into it the breath of life.

In paragraph 6200 of *Arcana Coelestia*, Swedenborg describes a kind of experience that takes us from the physical to the mental level, and brings us explicitly into the wave domain:

> Since I have been constantly in the company of an-
> gels and spirits for nine years now, I have carefully
> observed how influx works. When I thought, the
> concrete images of thought seemed to be in the
> middle of a kind of wave, and I noticed that this
> wave was simply all the matters associated in my
> memory with the topic of the thought. This meant
> that the whole thought was perceptible to spirits,
> though nothing came through to human senses but
> the matter that was in the center and seemed to be
> concrete.

This fascinates me in part because of its identification of waves as carriers of information. Current technology has made this a commonplace, and I find it most promising as an image of mental processes. I would also put it together with another image which I think of as Swedenborg's epistemology in a nutshell. It is from the first paragraph of *Soul-Body Interaction*:

> Since the soul is spiritual substance, and by reason
> of order is more pure, more primary, and more in-
> ward, while the body is material and therefore
> more crude, more secondary, and more outward,
> and since it is in keeping with order for the more
> pure to flow into the more crude, the more primary
> into the more secondary, and the more inward into
> the more outward, it is therefore in keeping with
> order for the spiritual to flow into the material, and
> not the reverse.

This means that the thinking mind flows into the sight, subject to the state imposed on the eyes by the things that are being seen—a state which that mind, further, arranges at will. In the same way, the perceiving mind flows into the hearing, subject to the state imposed on the ears by words.

If I put these two passages together, I have a picture of myself as a mental entity being constituted by the intersection of two flows of waves. One, which we might conveniently label the subjective flow, comes into my consciousness from within. The other, which we may label the objective flow, comes into my consciousness from the outside, through my senses. My consciousness itself looks very much like an interference pattern which cannot be defined without due reference to both sources. I am neither wholly self-defining nor wholly determined by my circumstances. As a perceiver, I do construct my perceptions, but I do so out of available materials. I live in a kind of no man's land between ontology and epistemology.

In Swedenborg's view, both of these flows originate in the Divine. If I were to diagram them, I could do worse than simply to take the diagram of how one makes a holo-gram—there is the flow from the single source, its division into direct and indirect flows, and their meeting in an inter-ference pattern that is the carrier of meaning.

This does radical things to my assumptions about my-self as a discrete entity. My usual image is of a kind of par-ticle, with distinct boundaries and with an absolute differ-ence between the things that are inside me and the things that are outside me. Introspection and looking outward are quite separate undertakings, as are caring for myself and caring for others. If I feel that my identity is threatened, the immediate reaction is to defend my borders, to claim my contents as exclusively mine and as being of value. At my best, I may be willing to admit that your contents are yours and are also of value, but I will do this only if I am fairly se-cure about mine. It is easy for me to ignore the fact that my opinions of other people reveal a great deal about me.

In the holographic model, there are no such fixed boundaries. Waves have amplitude and frequency, and they do decay more or less rapidly depending on the vis-cosity of the medium; but as mentioned, they combine with each other with the greatest of ease. If I visualize myself as an interference pattern, I am first of all aware that this is sim-ply an area of a far larger pattern. I realize that things that are "outside" me at one time are "inside" me at another, that I can for example distance myself from "my own" ideas or values, that "I" can at times seem quite alien to "myself."

I also become aware of the wisdom of the view that the human being is a microcosm, that there is a universe within that reflects the universe without, no matter where one draws the line between the within and the without. Again,

Swedenborg takes note of this, for example in paragraph 6057 of *Arcana Coelestia*: " . . . the inner person is a miniature heaven and the outer person a miniature world—a microcosm."

This principle is stated explicitly only a few times, but it is integral to his view of salvation. In paragraph 420 of *Heaven and Hell,* for example, there is the statement that "every single individual is born for heaven—people are accepted if they accept heaven into themselves and are shut out if they do not." In paragraphs 203. of the same work, this idea is further developed: "To the extent that anyone is in the form of heaven, he or she is in heaven, and is in fact a heaven in smallest form."

There are people who believe that thoughts and affections do not really reach out around them, but are within them. This is because they see within themselves, not farther away, the things they are thinking about. They are quite mistaken, however. For just as eyesight has an outreach to remote objects, and responds to the arrangement of the things it sees in that outreach, so the more inward sight proper to the understanding has an outreach in the spiritual world.

Or again *(Arcana Coelestia* n. 3633):

> Further, heaven as a whole is of such nature that each individual is like a center of all. In consequence, an image of heaven is reflected in each individual and makes that individual like itself—that is, a person. The nature of the inclusive whole in fact determines the nature of the part of the whole, since the parts must be like their whole in order to belong to it.

One last quotation from *Arcana Coelestia* n. 7270 is appropriate, with a brief comment on it, before I summarize:

> . . . there are connected stages from the First (that is, from the Lord) all the way to the last things, which are in humanity, and to the very last things which are in nature. The last things in humanity, like those in nature, are relatively dark and therefore cold, and are relatively general and therefore hazy. We can see from this that through these stages there is a constant connection of all things with the first Reality. Inflow is patterned by these stages, for the divine-true that emanates directly from the divine-good flows in by stages, and in its course, or at each new stage, it becomes more general and therefore coarser and hazier, and it becomes slower, and therefore more viscous and colder. . . .

But we must be precisely aware that the divine-true which flows into the third heaven (nearest the Lord) also flows without sequential adaptation into the last elements of the pattern, and from that First directly governs and oversees everything there. This is what holds the stages together in their pattern and coherence.

The truth of this can in some measure be confirmed by principles that scholars are aware of—that substance proper is simply unique, that all other things are secondary formations, and that that unique substance rules in all the formations. . . .

Matter, in this view, is seen not as solid but as "viscous." Relative to our mental processes, it moves so slowly that it seems to be permanent. Geological changes, even physiological changes in our own bodies, are constant but rarely noticed. We are constantly redrawing our physical boundaries.

To summarize, then, the fact of the hologram enables us to lift out of the mass of Swedenborg's theological corpus a consistent theme centering in the image of intersecting flows. This theme stands in complementary relationship to the more usual view of reality as consisting of discrete parts. Explicitly holographic statements occur as early as *Arcana Coelestia* and as late as *Divine Love and Wisdom.*

Next, I will be looking at the impact of this theme in Christology in particular, and I would now suggest only that the holographic model has a direct and obvious pertinence to the question of the nature of plurality in oneness. In my concluding paper, I will be dealing with some ethical implications; and at that point I hope it will become clear that this view is less far out than it may at first seem, that in fact it touches directly on very ordinary experience.

Christian Theology
and
the Holographic Model

Part II
Christology

At the close of Part I, I suggested that "the holographic model has a direct and obvious pertinence to the question of the nature of plurality in oneness." Swedenborg's metaphysical stance in this is perhaps best summed up in paragraph 14 of *Divine Love and Wisdom*:

> Where there is Reality [Esse], there is Presence [Existere]: neither occurs apart from the other. Reality actually exists through Presence, and not apart from it. . . . They are distinguishably one, like love and wisdom. Love, further, is Reality, and wisdom is Presence, since love occurs only in wisdom, and wisdom only from love. So when love is in wisdom, it then has presence. These two are one in such a way that they can be distinguished in

> thought, but not in fact; and since they can be dis-
> tinguished in thought and not in fact, we therefore
> refer to them as "distinguishably one."

I now understand this statement largely in terms of wave-particle duality, seeing love as a wave property, so to speak, and wisdom as a particle property. It is characteristic of love to unite, and characteristic of wisdom to distinguish; and Swedenborg would insist that unity is meaningless unless the parties to the union retain their integrity. "A form is the more perfect," he writes, "as the elements entering into it are distinctly different, and yet united" (*Divine Providence* n. 4 [4]). Otherwise, the outcome is confusion and distortion rather than genuine oneness.

To focus for the moment on the distinguishability, the duality of love and wisdom is central to Swedenborg's thought in general and to his Christology in particular. In metaphysical terms, he sees the trinity as a trinity of love, wisdom, and the effect of their union. In good holographic fashion, he sees this trinity reflected everywhere—in human action as the product of human intention (or love) and human thought, for example, or in inanimate objects as consisting of substance and form. I might mention that while Swedenborg rarely refers to "law" and "grace" in their common Christian usage, it seems clear that he would regard grace as a feature of love, and law as a feature of wisdom, and would therefore see them as "distinguishably one."

I really do not know how much attention to give to this concept for present purposes. It has been central to my own thinking since I started thinking. I heard it from Reuben Walker, the carpenter who was one of my early

Sunday School teachers, and it is hard for me to regard it as elusive or arcane; though I do find it missing in much of what I read or hear from other traditions. If it is not clear at this point, I hope it will become more so as it recurs in different contexts in what follows.

I would move from this to Christology by way of one of Swedenborg's descriptions of the nature of love (*Divine Love and Wisdom* n. 47).

The central characteristic of love is not loving oneself, but loving others, and being united to them through love. The central characteristic of love is being loved by others, and so being in fact united. The essence of all love consists of union—this is in fact its life, which is called joy, charm, delight, sweetness, blessedness, contentment, and happiness. Love consists in having one's own belong to another and in feeling another's joy as joy in oneself: that is loving. But feeling one's own joy in another and not the other's in oneself is not loving: this is loving oneself; the other is loving the neighbor.

I would call particular attention to the fact that the self-other distinction remains intact in this union, that the joy felt within oneself can be recognized as the joy of the other. This is seen as applying to God's love for us as well as to our love for each other. To quote from *True Christian Religion* n. 504 (5–7):

> A human being is an organ of life, and God alone is life. God pours his life into the organ and all its parts, as the sun pours its warmth into a tree and all its parts. Further, God grants people a sense that the life in them seems to be their own. God wants us to have this sense, so that we may live in appar-

ent independence, according to the laws of the [divine] design . . . and may thus dispose ourselves to accept the love of God. Yet God continually keeps his finger on the vertical tongue of the balance, so to speak, to keep it within bounds, but never violates our free choice by compulsion. . . . Our free choice results from the fact that we have a sense that the life we enjoy belongs to us.

This principle is stated in extreme form in *Soul-Body Interaction* n. 14:

God alone acts: we let ourselves be acted upon, and react to all intents with apparent independence, though this too, more inwardly, comes from God.

In this context, the central problem of Christology is not how Jesus can be God or can be fully one with the Father; it is how we can not be. It involves the philosophical problem of understanding how the finite can coexist with the infinite, how I can exist as "not-God" without being a boundary or limit of God. Swedenborg, incidentally, handles this Gordian knot in good Gordian fashion in *True Christian Religion* n. 33:

The common notion is that since a finite entity cannot contain the infinite, finite things cannot be receptive of the infinite. But it follows from what I have published about creation that God first finited his infinity by means of substances emitted from himself. . . .

That is, God is seen to be intrinsically self-limiting. In more human terms, we exist because divine love wants us to and divine wisdom is capable of distinguishing us. I doubt that any mechanical or strictly mathematical notion of infinity can substitute for the concept of love in maintaining and dealing with the finite-infinite paradox.

Incarnation, then, or the real presence of the infinite in the finite, is a wholly characteristic divine act. The specialness of the presence of God in Christ is not a matter of kind for Swedenborg but a matter of degree. We dimly reflect the presence of the Divine within us—some people more, some less. Jesus so completely reflected that presence that if we want to know what in us reveals and what obscures that presence, we have an archetype to look to. I believe that we err if we try to make the incarnation special by making it different in kind from all other acts of God. If it is a revelation of the nature of the Divine, it should surely be an act characteristic of that nature.

To me, this is where the holographic model is directly useful. It is wholly characteristic of the Divine to be wholly present in every part of creation, all the time. There is really no problem of "who was running the universe while God was in Christ," except as the situation is seen solely in the "particle" image. Whether one takes the Virgin Birth literally or not, as an image of the Divine operating directly into a secondary matrix it is a fundamental image of the way everything happens.

The holographic model is useful also in another respect. Because waves can superimpose on each other without losing their integrity, a single plate can record a sequence of images. As the observer moves in relation to the image, the image "moves." Time, so to speak, is condensed into total simultaneity in the plate and can be reconstructed from that simultaneity without loss of the integrity of the sequential stages.

Looked at from a slightly different perspective, this means that the information recorded on the holographic plate and existing there all together and all at once can be understood only in a sequence of images over a span of time. And this, of course, is how God is presented to us in Christ—in a sequence of images over a span of time.

Swedenborg's Christology is above all a process Christology. He writes in *True Christian Religion* n. 73 (3):

> God could not use his omnipotence to rescue us except by becoming human; and he could not make his human divine except by having his human be first like the human of an infant, then like that of a child, and later by having made that human form itself into a vessel and dwelling into which the Father could enter. This was accomplished by his fulfillment of all things of the Word—that is, all the laws of the [divine] design that it contains. To the extent that he did accomplish this, he made himself one with the Father, and the Father made himself one with him.

This process is seen as involving an alternation of states which is related directly to the concept of "distinguishable oneness." The Gospels portray Jesus as sometimes intensely conscious of his oneness with the Father, and sometimes intensely conscious of separation. The "same person" could say both, "Anyone who has seen me has seen the Father," and "My God, my God, why have you abandoned me?" Swedenborg comments in *True Christian Religion* n. 105:

> The reason the Lord had these two states, one of emptiness and one of glorification, was that this was the only way he could progress toward becoming one, since this is in accord with the divine design, which is unchangeable. The divine design is that we should arrange ourselves to accept God and prepare ourselves as vessels and dwellings into which God may enter, and where he may live as in his temple.

We are to do this in apparent independence, still acknowledging that it all comes from God. We are to acknowledge this because we do not feel God's presence and working, even though God is most intimately accomplishing everything that is good in love and everything that is true in faith. Everyone moves and must move according to this design in order to become spiritual instead of [merely] physical.

The Lord moved in the same way in order to make his natural human divine. This is why he prayed to the Father, why he did his will, why he credited everything he did and said to the Father, and why he said on the cross, "My God, my God, why have you abandoned me?" In this state God does indeed seem to be absent.

But after this state there comes another, a state of union with God. In this latter state we act as before, but we are then acting from God. There is no longer any need to credit God with everything good that we intend and do and everything true that we think and say, because this is written on our hearts, and is therefore inherent in our every action and word.

This is how the Lord united himself to his Father, and the Father united him with himself. In a word, the Lord glorified his human (that is, made it divine) the way the Lord regenerates us (that is, makes us spiritual).

The self-image I have of a present consciousness encased in a particular body is a necessary and useful one, but by itself it is not an adequate image of my humanity. It overlooks the extent to which my past is present in me, the extent to which I am a human in process. It is equally suspect to regard the incarnation as the presence of the Divine simply in a human shape, and not in that human process. Again, the holographic model helps me to see that process as the sequential experience of a design that exists simultaneously, and I believe that something like this underlies Swedenborg's statement that "this was the only way [Jesus] could progress toward becoming one, since this is in accord with the divine design, which is unchangeable" (*True Christian Religion* n. 105).

Swedenborg also wrote in considerable detail about the process of glorification. It is not easy material even for people familiar with his style and vocabulary, but there is fortunately an easier means of access to an outline of the process. As already suggested, this process is seen as differing from ours in scale or degree rather than in kind. He writes in *Arcana Coelestia* n. 3296:

96

> That is, we can see in [our own] regeneration, as in
> a kind of image, how the Lord glorified his human,
> or made it divine, which is the same thing. Just as
> the Lord wholly changed his human state into a
> divine one, so in us, when he is regenerating us, he
> wholly changes our state, for he makes the old per-
> son into a new one.

I would suggest that this is most understandable as a statement that there is a basic sequence inherent or implicit in the simultaneous design, and with that observation would turn to some presentations of that sequence. Swedenborg's classic statement occurs at the very begin-ning of his first published theological work, *Arcana Coelestia* nn. 6–13:

> 6. The six days or times, which are six successive
> states of human rebirth, are in general like this.

> 7. The first state is the one that precedes—both the
> state from infancy and the state just before rebirth.
> It is called void, emptiness, and darkness. And the
> first motion, which is the Lord's mercy, is the spirit
> of God hovering over the face of the water.

> 8. The second state is when a distinction is made
> between the things that are the Lord's and the
> things that belong to the person. The things that are
> the Lord's are called "the remnants" in the Word,
> and are primarily insights of faith which have been
> learned from infancy. These are stored away and
> do not surface until the person reaches this state,
> which rarely happens nowadays without trial, mis-
> fortune, or depression, which deaden the physical

and worldly concerns that are typically human. In this way, the concerns of the outer person are separated from those of the inner. The remnants are in the inner person, stored away there by the Lord for this time and for this use.

9. The third state is one of repentance, in which the individual, from the inner person, does talk reverently and devoutly and does bring forth good [actions], that resemble deeds of charity. Still, they are not really alive because they are thought to be done independently. They are called the tender plant, the seed-bearing plant, and finally the fruit tree.

10. The fourth state is when the individual is moved by love and enlightened by faith. Before this, the person did indeed talk reverently and bring forth good [actions], but out of a state of trial and constraint, not out of faith and charity. So now faith and charity are kindled in the inner person, and are called the two great lights.

11. The fifth state is when the person talks from faith and consequently strengthens his or her devotion to what is true and good. The things now brought forth are live, and are called the fish of the sea and the birds of the air.

12. the sixth state is when the person says what is true and does what is good from faith and therefore from love. The things now brought forth are called the living soul and the animals. And since the individual is then beginning to act from both faith and love, he or she becomes a spiritual person, who is called an image. The spiritual life of such an individual is delighted and nourished by things

related to insights of faith and to works of charity,
which are called "food"; and the natural life is delighted and nourished by things related to the body
and the senses. This results in conflicts until love
gains control, and the person becomes heavenly
[the seventh state].

13. Not all people who are being reborn reach this
state. Some—most people nowadays—reach only
the first, some only the second. Some reach the
third, fourth, and fifth, few the sixth, and hardly
anyone the seventh.

I may mention in passing that I find considerable con-
sonance between this schema and Fowler's outline of the
stages of faith development, and would like to believe that
this is because both Fowler and Swedenborg are observing the same essential process. It should also be stressed
that this process is seen to happen "with infinite variety" (cf.
Arcana Coelestia n. 7236). It is presented in most general
terms, and is thematic rather than prescriptive.

In summary, I see the holographic model as implicit in
Swedenborg's theology, and as having a particular impact
on his Christology. In his view it is intrinsic to the divine
nature to be wholly present in every part of creation, and
especially clearly in human beings. The incarnation is an
utterly characteristic act, the best clue we have, if you will,
as to what is going on right now. It is presented to us as a
process, as a series of images over a span of time, since this
is the modality by which we may best grasp the unchang-
ing and simultaneous design from which it emerges.

Christian Theology
and
the Holographic Model

Part III
Ecclesiology and Ethics

The holographic model raises provocative questions about what is "mine" and what is "yours," and these lead directly into matters of both ecclesiology and ethics. Once there is an awareness of the validity and usefulness of wave images, it is clear by contrast how considerably church organizations, like most human organizations, rest in particle models. In varying degrees, they lay considerable stress on criteria for membership and assume that membership in one denomination precludes membership in another. Their internal structures are usually designed to mark off clear areas of responsibility with clear channels of communication and clear lines of authority. One extreme of this is the Catholic image of a world divided into sees which are divided into parishes, with a single Pope at the head. Extreme in another fashion are cults which try to isolate themselves completely from the rest of the world, often claiming that they alone are "saved" and that all others are "damned." *Extra ecclesiam [meam] nulla salus*—"Outside the [my] church there is no salvation."

It is not difficult to see that this latter attitude is at odds with the image that the Divine is wholly present everywhere. There may be no literal contradiction, since the divine presence does not necessarily equate with salvation, but I find it hard to conceive of a form of divine presence that does not at least offer the possibility of salvation.

Swedenborg is explicitly ecumenical in this regard, and his ecumenism goes well beyond the bounds of Christianity. In *Divine Providence* n. 326 he writes:

> Provision has been made by the Lord that there should be some form of religion almost everywhere; and provision has also been made by the Lord that everyone who acknowledges God and does not do wrong because it is against God should have a place in heaven. Heaven, taken all together, reflects a single person, whose life or soul is the Lord. In that heavenly person are all the components that exist in the natural person, the difference being like that between what is heavenly and what is natural. . . .

Heaven as a single person cannot be made up of the people of one religion—it needs people of many religions. So everyone who has made the two universal principles of the church [basically, for Swedenborg, the two great commandments] matters of life has a place in that heavenly person—that is, in heaven.

He also comments that ". . . gentiles from their religion think about God in their lives more than Christians do." (n. 322). As far as Swedenborg is concerned, *extra salutem nulla ecclesia*—"Apart from salvation, there is no church."

He remains, however, determinedly Christian. He gives a kind of overview of his rationale:

> That which makes heaven within a person also makes the Church, for theChurch is the Lord's heaven on earth. . . . That is called the Church where the Lord is acknowledged, and where the Word is; for the essentials of the Church are love to the Lord, and faith in the Lord from the Lord; and the Word teaches how a person must live in order to receive love and faith from the Lord. (*Arcana Coelestia*, n. 10760–1).

We define the church as being where the Lord is recognized and where the Word is present, since the essentials of the church are the Lord's gifts of love and faith in the Lord, and the Word teaches how we must live in order to accept love and faith from the Lord.

The Lord's church exists in internal and external forms. The internal church is in people who do the Lord's commandments from love, since these are the people who love the Lord. The external church is in people who do the Lord's commandments from faith, since these are the people who believe in the Lord.

People who are outside this church and who still recognize a single deity and live their religion in some form of charity toward the neighbor are in communion with people in the church, since no one who believes in God and lives well is damned. So we can see that the Lord's church is everywhere in the whole world, though it exists in its particular form where the Lord is recognized and where the Word is present.

I find this easiest to understand with the help of a wave model. Interference patterns can be very confusing as they become more intricate. If, however, one can discern one set of component waves, a pattern can begin to make sense. This means that a change in vantage point can make a real difference. Swedenborg takes Christianity to be that central vantage point from which the whole pattern can be most clearly seen. It should, in this view, be the religion which most clearly sees and most deeply appreciates the possibilities of salvation provided by God in all other religions. I should be a Christian rather than, say, a Buddhist because (my) Christianity appreciates (my) Buddhism more than (my) Buddhism appreciates (my) Christianity. This is a corollary of seeing the incarnation as the archetypical instance of what the Divine is always doing everywhere.

Our own denomination, incidentally, has just reorganized itself along lines suggested by the holographic model. The various boards are given centers of interest rather than boundaries of interest, and provision is made for overlap of concerns. There are rarely tasks that are purely pastoral, for example, with no educational dimensions.

The planning that formed the context of this reorganization paid explicit attention to our own "intersective nature," and this may serve to move us from ecclesiology as such to more general matters of ethics. For this intersective image undercuts two extreme positions, namely belief in total individual responsibility and belief in total social determinism. Every individual is seen as constituted by two flows, one "from within" and one from "without." The effort to define a person by one flow only is like telling someone that Grand Central Station is on the corner of 42nd Street.

This points to a constant in human relations which I rarely hear mentioned. Given a situation which calls for change—say an impasse in my family—the one area in which I surely seem able to effect change is in myself. Further, such change is absolutely inevitable: it is only a question of the kind of change. That is, my consciousness now "contains" a new situation. My perceptions and thoughts and feelings are different than they were before the impasse arose. I have various options as to how I internalize the situation, how I interpret the intersection of this particular objective flow with my present subjective flow, but it is still a portion of that objective flow which, in part, constitutes me as a person.

But if this is the one area in which I can surely seem to effect change, by the same token, changes in me are changes in the people for whom I am part of the objective flow. I do make a difference. The only question is what kind of difference I make.

Many common models of this difference are, as I have noted in Part I, strikingly Newtonian. I exert pressure, I react, I occasion tension or friction. Images of language often portray words as vehicles whose contents are meaning, as though a little train chugged from my brain into yours and the cars dumped their loads there.

One obvious inadequacy of this model is that I do not lose the contents which are supposedly transferred. Current cognitive research is helpful here, insisting that most words refer to mental categories rather than to "objective things" or events directly, that language reflects mind in its interpretations, its necessary simplifications, of the bewilderingly complex continuum of the objective flow.

Under the holographic model, I am not "putting any content" into your mind. I am using an arbitrary but accepted system of language to represent particular features of an overall pattern in which we are all participants. The effect I want is poorly represented by the image of a numerical increase in the number of your data. It is much better described as the phenomenon of "recognition"—a word which nicely implies previous acquaintance, or as "discovery," if that is taken rather literally as the uncovering of something that is already there.

I might mention that for me, this connects closely with the process or developmental models I mentioned in Part II. The actual interference pattern in which we participate is overwhelmingly complex, so much so that our senses and our minds are better conceived of as selectors or screens or simplifiers than as real perceptors or receptors. The cognitive side of spiritual development can then be viewed as involving different kinds of pattern perceived in the total field, with all the patterns "really there," so to speak, but some more inclusive and fundamental than others.

To return to the main theme, though, as I begin to accept the image that what is happening as you read is not so much the transfer of content from one mind to another as it is the representing of particular patterns in a reality which includes us all, the line between "what is mine" and "what is yours" becomes largely irrelevant. Just as part of my objective flow has been provided by the minds of Swedenborg, Bohm, Pribram, Grof, and Fowler, I am currently trying to be the central feature of your objective flow. In face to face conversation, you would be part of mine, and I would be trying so to focus on your words that you would be central.

In any case, the "you" that I responded to would be the "you" that I perceived, which means that it would be the "you" within me. I may habitually perceive you as quite other than myself; and while there is some truth in this, it can get me into trouble if I take it too literally. It makes it very easy for me to think that I have responded to you when in fact I have responded to my image or perception of you. I am better off if I recognize that there may be no ontological boundaries between us, that there may be only epistemological or cognitive boundaries, drawn for the convenience of our finite minds, and not always equally appropriate. Ideally, I should be as capable of disidentifying and identifying with you as I am with "myself"—whatever that is—or with any aspect of myself. This, for me, is coming to be the import of Jesus' prayer that the disciples might be one in the same way that he was one with the Father.

This does indeed raise some serious questions about that persistent problem, "my identity." In the holographic model, there is a single, all-inclusive pattern which models the infinite in the peculiar sense of transcending internal boundaries. Rightly viewed, any part represents the whole, which incidentally reminds me of the theory that I am created in the image and likeness of God. I know that my consciousness expands and contracts, that sometimes "I" am quite alien to "myself." I know that there is a kind of normal range of this expansion and contraction, and that there are rare moments when I move beyond that normal range in one direction or the other. I really can no longer define myself by my boundaries.

Instead, I begin to be aware that what is unique about me is where I am centered in the total pattern. This image of a center of identity calls to mind statements Swedenborg makes about "the inmost," such as the following from *Arcana Coelestia* n. 2973 (4):

> . . . our inmost [of an individual] is where the Lord dwells within us; and from there the Lord governs what lies round about. When we let the Lord arrange these surrounding things so that they are responsive to the inmost ones, then we are in a state in which we can be accepted into heaven, and then the inmost, the relatively inward, and the outward aspects [of our being] act as one.

Swedenborg elsewhere (*Last Judgment* n. 25, for example) insists that this inmost is beyond our reach, and remains intact as the inner source of life even with people in the deepest hells. He sees it, in other words, as the eternal identity which remains constant through all the vicissitudes of growth or decline.

Whenever I am aware that I am more a center than a strictly bounded area or invariant particle, it comes as an immense and practical relief. There is simply no need of defensiveness or of self-effacement—this new kind of identity seems inherently secure and grants the same measure of security to others. In a quite unexpected way, it seems also to make it much easier to accept responsibility, perhaps because "demands" are no longer experienced as coming solely from some alien source "out there."

I want to extend this model, though, into the general area of social ethics, and would begin by noting that the holographic model requires a fresh look at the significance of size or scale. To put it most bluntly, if I want a general overview of the world situation without getting lost in details, I should look at the microcosm—myself. If I want a detailed understanding of some particular facet of myself, I should look outward, at the macrocosm.

Let me illustrate this with a couple of examples. One of my favorite descriptions of the Christian menace is "He's a man who lives for others. You can tell the others by their hunted look." I met one of those a few years ago, immensely earnest and misinformed, and I found it impossible to reach any kind of mutuality. I was profoundly uncomfortable all the while I was trying to maintain appropriately constructive behavior. Introspectively, it was difficult for me to sort out my feelings: I would keep thinking of things I ought to say or should have said, or of inconsistencies between what he said and how he said it.

Looking outward at the global predicament, though, there was a quite obvious and precise image in the mushroom cloud. I really did not want this person to be. I could tell myself that I just wished he weren't there, but that was merely a socially acceptable disguise for wishing he were not in my world. For the first time in human history, we have a clear picture of the ultimate goal, the essential quality, of our everyday callousness.

To illustrate the other direction of search for understanding, I would draw on my attitude toward what we sometimes summarize as "the Pentagon." Especially in a profession where violence is normally limited to obliquely caustic footnotes, it is easy to condemn the whole military effort because of the obvious folly of particular details.

In fact, though, it is not that easy to generalize responsibly. No one would say that the anti-nuclear movement has won, and yet nuclear weapons have not been used in combat for more than forty years, for a full biblical generation. Something seems to have gone right, and the anti-nuclear movement surely cannot claim all the credit.

I begin to see a comprehensible pattern when I look inside. I realize that a part of me is a kind of "military mind"—a mind which wants clear and definite distinctions, orderly sequences and procedures, a mind which is irritated by people who drive fifty-three miles an hour in the middle lane of the highway. It is a mind which appreciates the precision of *Robert's Rules of Order* and is impatient when the chair lets the meeting ramble on forever without accomplishing anything, a mind which is tickled by the fact that this particular "Robert" is General Henry M. Robert, U. S. Army. It is a mind that recognizes that sometimes I can't persuade myself: sometimes I just have to give myself an order and follow it.

It is also a mind that I have to watch out for. Despite the foregoing, I do allow people to give me hugs without asking recognition from the chair, I do value brainstorming sessions where the application of Robert's Rules would be disastrous.

This "military mind" emerges as an invaluable servant and a tyrannical master. It is to be cultivated and appreciated, and to be used decisively whenever and wherever it is needed. What I have to watch is both my tendency to ignore it when it is needed and to let it loose when it is not.

I wind up, then, taking a second look at my attitude toward the Pentagon, with the general assumption that wholesale condemnation is as unwarranted and destructive as uncritical approval. Such condemnation contributes to a dynamic of polarization which is profoundly antithetical to peace. Denying the legitimate functions of the military simply evokes a more adamant defense of its legitimate and non-legitimate functions alike. Appalling boondoggles and draconic armament levels are justified by generalizations about our need for military strength. To look for a moment at an intermediate scale, the dynamic of polarization leads ultimately to a choice between living in a police state or living in a state without police.

I need to remind myself that these references to global matters are, for present purposes, illustrations. They are designed to lend some substance to the proposition that we are sufficiently microcosms that any absolute self-other dichotomy is false and hurtful, that even the I-Thou distinction has its dangers.

I would conclude by noting that much of what Swedenborg has to say about this is found in his discussions of proprium and to appropriate. Without going into detail, I would suggest that his proprium means approximately "what we regard as our own," and in the holographic model stands out as the boundaries we draw around ourselves. Swedenborg states at one point (*Arcana Coelestia* 154) that "nothing evil and false exists which is not proprium and from proprium," but shortly before that, he has made some significant qualifications. I quote from paragraph 141 of *Arcana Coelestia*, translating proprium as "self-image":

> In people who are occupied with physical and worldly concerns, their self-image is all that matters, is all they know. They think that if this self-image were lost, they would die. The self-image looks much the same in spiritually minded people, for while they admit and state that the Lord is the life of all, the giver of intelligence and wisdom, of thinking and acting, they don't really believe it. Heavenly minded people realize that the Lord is the life of all, the giver of thinking and acting, because they perceive that that is the way it is, and they have no craving for a self-image. Still, they are given one by the Lord, a self-image that brings with it a full perceptiveness of what is good and true, and a full measure of happiness.

In a sense, then, perhaps the central ethical import of the Swedenborgian version of the holographic model is to point to the possibility of moving beyond the need to define ourselves by excluding others, which for me gives a particular clarity to the injunction that I love my neighbor as myself.

Quality Time

A medical doctor, Larry Dossey, has written a book called *Space, Time, and Medicine* (Boston: Shambala, 1985). In it, he notes how seriously tension can affect our health, and how much our sense of time has to do with tension. He traces this to the concept of time as an invariable, mechanical reality, and goes on to explain that people have not always held this view.

Before precise mechanical timepieces were invented, people organized their lives much more by the natural events of light and dark, the seasons, the tides, and the like. Some of these were quite predictable, some were less so. Even though sunset itself is highly regular, it gets dark earlier on a cloudy day than on a clear one. Further, one event tended to shade into another. The tides come and go gradually. Spring can come slowly. There is a kind of "cushion" that is very different from the sound of the alarm clock going off at exactly seven o'clock, or the dentist's appointment at 10:15. This "cushion" enabled people to work more at their own pace, to take a little extra time to finish what needed to be done.

This kind of time was also cyclical. Mechanical time

passes by and never returns. But day follows day, spring follows spring, tide follows tide. If you miss one for some reason, there will be another. The consequences of missing the season may be severe, it is true. There may not be enough food stored for the winter, or it may be too late to plant for a full harvest. But if one can see it through, there will be another opportunity. The time will come around again.

In a way, this all changed beginning with the book of Exodus, which records the command that the date of the passover was to be marked as the beginning of the year (Exodus 12:2). The first passover was the moment of deliverance from slavery in Egypt. It was a unique event. It stood as a point from which time could be measured in a straight line, so to speak, generation after generation.

As the generations passed, there was the risk that the event would be forgotten. So the Bible states on occasion that the present generation actually participated in those past events. So Joshua says to the assembled tribes, "For the Lord our God, he it is that brought us up and our fathers out of the land of Egypt," even though the people that actually left Egypt had died in the wilderness.

Now, of course, we measure time more accurately than it has ever been measured before. Ordinary digital stopwatches are calibrated in hundredths of a second and are accurate within a few seconds a month. Expensive ones, of course, may be better. And all of this does not seem to have made us much happier. We may be more efficient—presumably we could be—but there is something basic missing.

That something is the quality of the time, rather than the

quantity. Passover was the time of deliverance, and beginning the year with it was intended to begin the year with a consciousness of Divine grace. It was a reminder of national destiny, and therefore a reminder of the purpose of their existence. It called them to a renewed sense of obligation to the covenant on which their security depended. It gave them a sense of direction.

We are told that after death it may be possible to review our lives and to see the consistent working of the Lord's providence in them. We may be quite sure that events will stand forth with unexpected meaning. We may be quite sure that our sense of time will be very different. We will see a pattern joining things that seemed unrelated. We will wonder at our past impatience, because we will see that there was simply no way to hurry the process.

If we could see that providence now, it would have a similar effect. The pace of things would appear to be exactly right. We might be able to change it some, in fact, because we would be able to attend to critical tasks that we are unaware of and are therefore neglecting. But if we could see what is happening, we would find ourselves content with the Lord's care.

Changing circumstances have brought a new and useful phrase into our vocabulary—"quality time." With increase in the number of families in which both parents are working, there has been anxiety about the welfare of the children. Somewhat to the surprise of the researchers, it turns out that the amount of time parents spend with their children is somewhat less significant than is the quality of that time. The mother who is at home, but who is too busy to pay much attention to the child, can easily communicate to the child that he or she is an annoyance. The mother who works, if she can be genuinely glad to see the child, communicates a sense of love and worth.

The coming year will have the usual number of days, each with the usual number of hours in it. What we do with those days and hours is another matter entirely. The medical model that is currently under question attends almost exclusively to the numbers. It is better to live longer, even though the life be sustained by machines, and be completely unproductive.

We really do know better. We do not follow this principle in our own lives. When we talk about our "good days" and our "bad days," we are not talking about their length. We know that a long summer day is not "better" than a short winter one, that the value of a day depends on what we do with it.

Was last year a good one? In order to evaluate it, we need to examine what use we made of it. What have we learned? What has happened to our relationships to each other? What is our sense of the Lord's guidance, and how has it changed?

Will next year be a good one? We have little control over much of what will happen to us. We do not know what will go smoothly and what will lead into difficulties. We do know that we will be left free to respond, and that the essential "goodness" of the coming year will depend on our responses.

The Lord will, in His providence, be offering us choices. Sometimes they will be choices between different actions. Sometimes we will not have much choice as to what we do—we pretty much have to pay the bills, take care of the house, and so on—but we will still have a choice as to the spirit in which we do them. There are people who do everything they are supposed to and seem to hate every minute of it. They are depressing people to be around.

We cannot see what the Lord has in store for us. We can be assured only that it comes from His love for us and His understanding of our needs. If we do the best we can, we will be brought nearer to heaven, and the coming year will be the best one yet.

The Progress Issue

I t may surprise Swedenborgians, talking especially to the clergy of other denominations, to discover that the idea of world spiritual progress is suspect. We are so accustomed to believe that the Lord has come and is leading us toward the fulfillment of His promises that denying the fact or the possibility of progress seems like a lack of faith, like a denial of divine providence itself.

There are, however, historical reasons for this mistrust. At the close of the last century and the beginning of this one, optimism reigned supreme in Protestant Christianity. The Western world was immensely impressed with the triumphs of science. There was a general belief that in a very short time, all scientific questions would be answered—one eminent physicist was advising young men to go into some other field, because very shortly there would be nothing left to discover. Since this progress had happened in the context of Christendom, it was taken as a validation of that faith, and there was what strikes us now as an incredibly naive faith that Christianity would soon displace all other religions. When that happened, obviously all the problems of the world would be solved.

The First World War shook this attitude but did not destroy it. The right side won, evil was defeated. But then came the Depression, and then came the Second World War, with the Holocaust in Europe, a Christian area, and similar brutality in the Far East. The rose-colored glasses were shattered. In the mainline churches there was renewed attention to the doctrine of original sin. As one prominent theologian writes:

> The sharp contemporary awareness of the injustice, the exploitation, the inordinate self-concern, and thus the ultimate self-destruction of even modern, liberal scientific culture—the culture that was to eradicate precisely those characteristics of historical life—has, therefore, directly refuted the dream of progress and validated in a quite new way the traditional sense of a fallen, or at least a deeply troubled, history. An awareness of the poignant relevance (if not the truth) of the ancient symbolism of original sin—and of the need for rescue from somewhere or other—are very much a part of contemporary sensibility.

As the writer suggests, this is not necessarily a return to the doctrine of original sin that was so distasteful to Swedenborg. Swedenborg objected to the notion that we are born guilty, a notion that was regularly used to support the authority of the institutional church. He did not take a rosy view of human nature, insisting that we are born inclined to evils of every kind, and that without repentance, reformation of life, and regeneration, we confirm those evils in ourselves. He would surely applaud the recognition of the "poignant relevance (if not the truth) of the ancient symbolism of original sin,"especially the usefulness of the word "symbolism."

This points to a way to believe in providence and in progress without falling into the facile optimism of the turn of the last century. It enables us to recognize both that we have come a long way and that we have still a long way to go. It reminds us that progress is not inevitable, for any or for all of us; but it offers the assurance that progress is possible.

The Biblical grounds for this view are extensive and secure. In the historical books, the prophets, and the Gospels, we find promises of a blessed future as well as recognition of the fallen state of humanity. The more spectacular of these promises speak of some kind of direct divine intervention in human affairs, of a "day of the Lord" in which all evil will be destroyed, and these passages have captured the attention of some denominations.

But there is another kind of prophecy as well. There are images of a kind of organic growth. "In those days, and at that time, will I cause the Branch of Righteousness to grow up unto David; and he shall execute judgment and righteousness in the land." "And he said, So is the kingdom of God, as if a man should cast seed into the ground: And should sleep, and rise night and day, and the seed should spring and grow up, he knoweth not how."

This latter image especially suggests that we cannot judge progress simply by outward appearances. There is always something going on underneath the surface. The fact of exploitation is indeed significant, and not to be ignored. The very awareness of that fact is also significant. From our perspective, the optimists at the turn of the century were almost unbelievably naive, apparently blind to injustices on all sides. The will to recognize and to face problems has grown immensely in the last century.

This will has not been ineffective. On the global scale, colonial tyranny has to a considerable extent been eliminated. The patronizing attitude toward non-Christian religions no longer dominates, and native cultures are valued and respected. Wars have been limited and accompanied by insistent and often successful efforts at negotiation. There are early signs of change in the largest-scale international problem, the Cold War. There are probably more and larger warless areas on the globe at this time than at any time in this millennium.

On the national scene, civil rights have been extended significantly. Discrimination that was taken absolutely for granted at the beginning of the century is now faced and resisted. We have seen a President driven from office for practices that were once ignored. If we look at the patent medicine advertisements of times gone by, we can even say that there has been progress toward truth in advertising.

We may need to remind ourselves of all this, because we are acutely aware of the problems that we still face. The fact that we have come a long way does not mean that we are necessarily near the end of the journey. At this point, in fact, it seems as though every time injustice is faced and rejected in one form, it resurfaces in a more subtle form. The myth of the Hydra comes to mind—cut off one head, and two more grow in its place.

This should neither surprise nor dishearten us. Facing more subtle forms of evil is in itself an aspect of progress. We know this from our own lives, having overcome the blatant but superficial egoism of childhood, and discovering over the years more and more of its deeper roots. The mystics unanimously testify to the possibility of a "death of the ego," and Jesus used a particularly vivid imaged to describe his own intent—"And now also the axe is laid unto the root of the trees."

In the view of Swedenborgian theology, we are progressing toward the root of evil, and it seems clear that we have a long way to go. There is still the widespread illusion that self-interest can solve fundamental problems, that national pride will make us secure, that more lethal weapons will guarantee peace, that disciplined greed will lead to prosperity. As long as these and similar illusions persist, we will keep choosing courses of action that lead to tragedy; and we may expect that as in the past, we will then face those particular forms of evil and reject them.

The hope is that ultimately we will find ourselves willing to face the law of love squarely. We will, that is, admit that we have not been created to serve ourselves, but to serve each other. Our nation, if it still exists by then, will be secure because other nations are glad and grateful that it exists, because of what it contributes to the health and well-being of our world. Our economy will be healthy because individuals will be more concerned to contribute to it than to extract from it.

This sounds unrealistic, and that is a good thing. We must not forget that we have a long way to go, a very long way indeed. But we must also not forget that we have come a long way from the times when war was an accepted way of life, when it was taken for granted that military might should be used for conquest.

We must also beware of taking credit for this progress. We have been notably reluctant pilgrims on this journey. The improvements have not been made willingly, out of the goodness of our own hearts. It has taken disaster after disaster to convince us of the need to change.

In other words, it has taken the providence of God to lead us, step by painful step. The Biblical images of intervention, of cataclysm, are just as necessary as the images of organic growth. For the very fact that self-centeredness leads to disaster is an indication that the underlying order of creation is beneficent. There is a profound oneness that resists violation, that brings peace and health only when love and understanding flourish. There is an infinite, unfailing Source of the love which we need for our survival and which we are powerless to create. There is an inherent wisdom to the very design of our world and our universe, and that wisdom will inevitably make itself known as our choices are followed by consequences.

Our task is simply to do the best we can with whatever circumstances providence offers us, falling prey neither to facile optimism nor to disheartening pessimism—accepting the tasks the Lord gives us with the faith that they are necessary and that each one of us makes a difference.

Sorting Things Out

When it is evening, you say, It will
be fair weather: for the sky is red.
And in the morning, It will be foul
weather today: for the sky is red
and lowering. O hypocrites, you
can discern the face of the sky; but
can you not discern the signs of the
times?

Matthew 16:2–3

There are certainly times when this might strike us as an unfair question. Even if we just read the papers or watch the news, there are so many different "signs of the times" that it is hard to sort them out. There is a great deal of violence, injustice, and war, true; but currently there is also the collapse of the Iron Curtain, and the growth of a peaceable and cooperative European Community. If we add to these news items the experiences of our own daily lives, it may be no less confusing. We do not in fact often encounter the violence we read about. We meet with some

125

inconsiderateness, some thoughtlessness, some unfairness, but we also meet with affection and understanding. We have no real way to tell which predominates in our world, no way to keep score.

It is tempting to compare our times with former times, but this too is not as easy as it might seem. We read currently about child abuse, and talk about the breakdown of the family. *The New York Times Magazine* recently had a picture of a miner from the turn of the century—a grimy figure with his hard hat and his pick, smoking a briar pipe. He looked to be about seven years old. When we look back, we do not see what lies beneath the surface unless we do some serious research. There is every probability that our own children will look back on these years and remember them as good. No, it is not easy to "discern the signs of the times."

I am more and more convinced, though, that Swedenborgian theology can help us sort things out. All we need to do, in a sense, is to take its simple, basic assertions seriously and see what they imply. I want to do this with two of the most familiar ones—divine goodness and human freedom.

We believe that the Lord is utterly loving and wise, and omnipotent. This means that the strongest force in the universe is absolutely good. I suspect that most of the time, we see goodness as on the defensive in this world, and it certainly looks that way. But Swedenborgian theology says that this is only an "appearance," and a little reflection may help us realize how true this is.

We have our good side and our bad side. In part we really want to live good lives, but there are those times when we seem to lose it. If we look at those latter times, they come when something we value or cherish is threatened. We go on the offensive, that is, when we feel on the defensive. It may be on behalf of someone else or it may be for our own sake. The threat may be to something we possess, something we want, or simply to our own self-esteem. The fact remains that it is easiest to be caring and considerate when we are secure.

Let's take a simple and concrete example. You're driving the family somewhere and miss a turn. If you know the territory, this may be irritating, but you know what to do about it. You probably mutter something, get back on track, and pretty much forget about it. But if the territory is unfamiliar, the anxiety and irritation are more intense. You feel uncertain, not sure what to do. The fact is that you may be no farther off course than in the first instance. The solution may be very simple. But you don't know that. In other words, the threat is not so much the physical situation as it is the uncertainty, the insecurity.

Let's transfer that to something that goes a bit deeper. In much the same way, the hardest thing about raising children is not knowing what to do. What is a distressing problem with the first child may be no problem at all with the second. The problem itself may not be all that different, but our own attitude has changed.

Now let's make one last transfer and go as far as we can toward the Lord. Suppose that we had the fullest possible measure of that wisdom and love that rule the universe. Suppose that we saw clearly what needed to be done with every problem that we faced. And think now of how different all those problems would look to us. I suspect that we would move through life in a very gentle and peaceable way, simply because we would always see a promising way to respond. We wouldn't be distressed, say, when one of the children did or said something troubling, because we wouldn't have that awful feeling that things might be getting out of control or that we might blow it.

Our own negative side, then, seems to be very much on the defensive. Swedenborgian theology says that we can and should extend this to the world in general. All the things that are going wrong are reactions to people or situations that are seen as threatening.

This would be a hopelessly romantic view of life if we did not take into account human freedom and its consequences. It would not be enough simply to remove all the actual threats, because we are perfectly capable of seeing threats where there are none. The world is complex, and we have a wide range of choice in what we will focus on. Bit by bit, we build up habits of perception. A few years ago I had a fascinating ride with a couple of friends. One seems constitutionally sunny, and the other I think of as Eeyore. Give her the most beautiful spring day imaginable, and she'll say something like, "It's too bad this kind of weather never lasts." Listening to the two of them talk, it was hard to believe that they were both living in the same world.

If we step back and look at the bare physical facts, there is not much to be gained. Both of them are "right" in that respect. It may be the most beautiful spring day imaginable. It is equally true that it will not last forever. It does seem, though, that now is not the time to focus our attention on next winter's cold and slush. It may be a good time to do some work on the snowblower, but we can surely enjoy the warmth and sunshine while we do.

But there is another aspect of our freedom that is at least equally important. When we feel threatened, we are worried about what is going to happen. Usually, these anxieties are hard to deal with because they are vague. One of the main reasons the past looks better than the present is that we know how it turned out. We know we made it through. I recall one time years ago when it had been raining for several days, and we had that feeling that it would never stop. My father remarked that in his whole life, he had experienced only one period of rain that had not ended—which of course was the one we were in at the time.

Of course there will be some end to whatever problem we are facing at the moment. Of course we do not know what the outcome will be. But our freedom means that this outcome is not predestined. It makes a difference whether we respond constructively or not. We may not be able to make everything right, to get everything we want, but we can make things better or worse. If this seems idealistic, think of any situation you like, and I have no doubt that you can think of ways in which you could have made it worse. Simply not doing or saying those things is better than doing or saying them.

We do not welcome sickness, for example. But sickness can draw people closer together. It can awaken our better natures and stimulate us to care for each other. I even suspect that in the Lord's design for us, sickness will cease from our world not when we find cures for all our physical ailments, but when we care for each other so faithfully that we no longer need reminders.

This brings us back toward the place where we started, looking at our times in general. What are "the signs of the times"? In the first place, they are those things we can observe now which give us clues as to what is going to happen. When it is evening, you say, It will be fair weather: for the sky is red. And in the morning, It will be foul weather today: for the sky is red and lowring. Today does contain the seeds of tomorrow. When we look back to yesterday, we can often see what we missed, and understand why things turned out the way they did.

But more specifically, what are the signs of our own times? How do we understand what is going on? How do we find clues to where we are headed?

I would suggest that there is one critical question which we are all too likely to overlook— "What is the Lord up to?" When we stop to think about it, this is after all the main issue. Our own intentions are important, but in the last analysis they are reactions to the Lord's initiatives. Swedenborg wrote, "God alone acts: we only react."

Whether things are going well or badly for us, there is something the Lord is trying to accomplish. The problems that arise are not new initiatives, but hidden things coming to the surface. If we use the image of our physical health, we regard ourselves as sick when we experience the symptoms of disease, but the most dangerous diseases are the ones that get out of control before the symptoms appear. At a regular medical check-up, the doctor is literally "looking for trouble." We may be quite sure that if more people had "looked for trouble" a generation ago, we would have far less trouble now. The signs were there, but only a few noticed them. What Rachel Carson was saying years ago about our ecological folly in *The Silent Spring* now seems painfully obvious, but at the time, it was highly controversial.

The social problems we face at present are symptoms. The Lord is trying to motivate us to do something. I suspect he is trying to bring us to admit that we have not created a country where there is liberty and justice for all. I am sure that he is urging us to look into our own hearts, to ask ourselves honestly how much we care about each other. He is asking us to recognize that mutual affection and understanding are more important goals, even more practical goals, than national prosperity or prestige. We may not like the signs of the times any more than we like the symptoms of disease; but as we come to believe that a wise and loving Lord is in control, we may be grateful for the signs. If we will, we can see what we have to deal with, and that is step one toward dealing with it.

Sell All You Have

*If you want to be perfect, go, sell
everything you own and give to the
poor, and you will have treasure in
heaven: and come, follow me.*

Matthew 19:21

On the basis of passages like this, Christianity has tended to look at wealth with suspicion, even to regard wealth as intrinsically sinful. There is currently a widespread insistence that Christianity stands for the poor and the oppressed and against the oppressor. While the motives for such insistence may be praiseworthy, it is surely risky to take a stance against the oppressor when the Gospels explicitly tell us to pray for those who persecute us. Something seems to be out of order here.

Part of the problem, I would suggest, involves the risks inherent in making generalizations. Jesus was talking to one individual, one wealthy young man. He saw that the main spiritual obstacle this young man faced was his attachment to his wealth, and he prescribed a radical cure for this attach-

133

ment. That does not mean that all wealthy people, or even all wealthy young men, suffer from the same malady. In fact, some people of relatively slender means are more preoccupied with money, more possessive in spirit, than some who would seem to have much more to be possessive about. We cannot tell people's spiritual states from their bank balances. The rich are not necessarily greedy, nor are the poor necessarily generous. The rich are not necessarily materialistic, nor are the poor necessarily enlightened.

As long as we simply take the story literally, then, we are restricted to this area of ambiguity. It is only when we look at the spiritual intent of this story that we begin to see its universal application. To put the matter simply and in traditional Swedenborgian terms, the story requires us to give up our sense of merit. Our spiritual riches are our good intentions and our true understandings, and we are to give up any sense that we deserve credit for them.

It is not easy to give up our sense of worth. Through much of our early life, our self-esteem is a major force for good in our lives. We resist giving in to our worse impulses because we know that otherwise we couldn't live with ourselves. We make sacrifices because it helps us to maintain our self-respect. We are more hurt than we would like to admit when some good we have done goes unnoticed or seems unappreciated, when the merits of our suggestion are ignored, when we do not seem to matter. Somewhere down inside, there is a voice telling us that we are special, and there is a need to have that message confirmed by voices from the outside. The voice is telling us the truth, but we find it hard to believe it.

As long as that need for reassurance exists, we cannot

afford to "sell all that we have," because if we do, we simply become poor. That is, we become engulfed in feelings of worthlessness, feelings that undermine our efforts to live useful lives and that cut us off from open and loving relationships with each other. We have all met people who felt rotten about themselves, and it is painfully obvious that this is not a heavenly way to live. This is not the humility that the Lord wants of us.

It is actually a feeling that makes us quite vulnerable, and churches have used it to manipulate people into obedience. Some have done this by preaching hellfire and brimstone sermons, some by insisting that only the church can deliver us from our inborn guilt. But the Lord's intent (and the intent of Swedenborgian theology) is not to manipulate people into anything. It is to set us free.

So perhaps we should reconsider what it is that the rich young man is supposed to sell. What would first come to mind would be his splendid house, his barns, his flocks and herds, his elegant clothes, and the like. But the command is to sell everything, not just the expensive things. It includes the broken ploughs and the overaged horses, the stuff in the back of the closet and the stretches of land where nothing will grow.

In more spiritual terms, there is something in common between having a positive self-image and having a negative one, and quite obviously, it is that both are self-images. Whether we are mightily impressed with our virtues or profoundly depressed by our vices, we are all wrapped up in ourselves. It is easy enough to recognize this in other people—they don't seem to be able to pay any real attention to us except to worry about what we are thinking about them. They keep trying to impress us with their wisdom or righteousness, or they keep fishing for approval from us. You've probably heard the caricature of this: "But that's enough talk about me, let's talk about you for a while. What do you think of my new suit?"

Self-righteousness is lethal stuff. It is particularly lethal because it makes genuine virtues ugly and destructive. Marital fidelity, for example, can be truly beautiful. But when physical fidelity is used as a platform for disapproval, as a tower of personal superiority, our truly good and loving instincts are repelled. Something inside us knows that if fidelity leads to this kind of smugness, it should be avoided like the plague. Marital fidelity does not, of course, lead to a sense of superiority over others. That is simply the lie that self-righteousness tells, but it can tell it powerfully and persuasively.

If both positive and negative self-images are so problematic, then it would seem that the only way out would be to have either a neutral self-image or no self-image at all; and I think we may head in the right direction through a kind of combination of the two. Can we have no self-image at all? I suspect that our first instinct is to say no, but that is an oversimplification. There are certainly times when we simply forget ourselves. Think of the difference between watching a magnificent sunset and watching ourselves watch it. The one experience takes us out of ourselves, the other embroils us in cataloguing our own reactions. Whenever we are totally absorbed in something else, whether it is watching a sunset, reading a book, peeling a potato, or listening to a friend, we have no functioning self-image. To test this, we need only to think of the change that occurs if something does call our attention to ourselves. We lose our concentration instantly, it seems, and have to deal in some way with the distraction before we can again give our attention outside ourselves.

That may do for the "no self-image," but it is not enough. We know all too well that we need to recognize what is going on inside ourselves. We need to sort out our motivations and make our choices. There is a very true sense in which we can understand others only as we come to understand ourselves.

In this regard, I think the key word in Matthew 19:21 is the word, "possessions." When we take inventory of ourselves, we tend to regard everything we find within ourselves as our possession—this is not just how I feel, it is what I am. It is not just that I feel resentful, somehow I am that kind of person.

In doctrinal terms, this is appropriation, claiming something as our own, and it is identified as the source of all our woes. The "neutrality" we might cultivate is not ignoring the differences between the better and the worse things we find in ourselves, but remaining neutral about ourselves. This good impulse is not "mine," it is something that is being offered me. This evil impulse is not "mine," it is something that is being offered me. Each represents only a tiny fragment of what I am as a total person; and in fact there is so much more to that total person than I have experienced that I really do not know me very well. Further, I have no way of measuring the good and the evil impulses to see which are predominant. Even if someone is keeping score, the scoreboard is out of my sight.

This opens the path to a far more detached or disinterested self-knowledge. If I can be mindful of the feelings and thoughts that occur to me, I can become familiar with some of the patterns that tend to recur. I tend to enjoy languages, and the absurdities that languages keep presenting. Sometimes this is an asset, sometimes it gets me into trouble. In stressful situations, I tend to become quieter rather than more active. Sometimes this is appropriate and sometimes it is not. I am capable of shifting my concentration from one thing to another fairly readily, and therefore capable of forgetting things completely. The good traits and the bad ones, or the better ones and the worse ones, are equally worth knowing about. I should be neutral, then, in the additional sense that I should want equally accurate information about both.

To "sell all that we have," then, is not some kind of punishment for having too much. It is more like a release from a trap, deliverance from attachment to our self-image, from worrying about ourselves, from the futile cycle of praise and blame. It may seem forbidding at first, because our immediate reaction is that we are being asked to give up our affirmative self-image only, and we would dearly like to think that, spiritually, we do have "great possessions." But if we are honest with ourselves, we realize that that affirmative image is a fragile one, shot through with uncertainty and demanding constant and expensive maintenance. Under its surface is an ugly suspicion—based on fact, but misusing fact—that it is all a fraud. Under its surface is a self-image that is as negative as the conscious one is affirmative; both are false, and that is why we are asked to give up both.

Lastly, this is precisely what the Holy Supper is all about, in a very different image. Our bodies are maintained by a constant intake and excretion of matter. That is, our bodies are matter flowing through us, as thoughts and affections flow through our minds. The physical food and drink of the sacrament may remind us that we are neither self-contained nor self-sustaining. Whatever we may find in ourselves that is good and true is a gift from the Lord, and not our possession. In doctrinal terms, we are not life, but recipients of life. That is what Scripture and doctrine are trying to tell us in countless ways, and it can strike just as deep as we will let it. The more the import of that simple statement sinks in, the more we find a truth that makes us free indeed.

The Spirit of Repentance

We aren't perfect. Sometimes we mean well but don't carry out our good intentions very effectively, and sometimes we "lose it" and don't mean very well at all. If we try to keep score, to figure out whether our helpful deeds and words outweigh our harmful ones, we find ourselves on the road to confusion. We have no idea how many points to award for this act, or how many to deduct from that one. There isn't a rule book that tells us how to keep score.

There isn't a rule book because that is not how spiritual life works. The important thing is that our decisions change our character and affect the lives of others. If there is a score, it is being kept in these changes, not in some account book in the sky.

In a way, then, the effects of our actions are not absolute. It is never too late to do something about them; and that is what repentance is all about. It is not trying to erase a black mark, it is trying to do something about the consequences of our wrongs.

There is no way we can change the past. All we can do in the present is either counteract it or reinforce it. So when we have erred, there is no particular point in berating our-

141

selves. It is quite natural but equally futile to call ourselves stupid or worthless, or to wallow in wishes that we had behaved differently. We did what we did, we said what we said, and that's it. Now we are in a new situation, a situation that includes our knowledge of what we have done. The present question is not whether we are going to do what we did. The present question is what we are going to do about it!

The worst thing we can do is to resort to self-justification or denial. We seem to have a remarkable ability to find reasons for what we have done, and to regard them as valid. We are helped by the fact that there is plenty wrong with the world around us. Other people are not perfect, either, and in the effort to excuse our own imperfections, we can always point to some wrong that has been done to us.

We may not notice that in doing this, we give up a measure of our own freedom. We claim, in effect, that circumstances left us no choice, that circumstances made us behave as we did. We give our surroundings power to make our decisions for us. "That makes me mad," is a very common and very dangerous statement, dangerous because it implies a lack of self-control.

The problem is that if we accept the freedom, if we acknowledge that we do have some control over our reactions to circumstances, we must also accept responsibility for our reactions, and that is precisely what we are trying to avoid in our self-justification and denial. We need to face the obvious fact that we cannot reject accountability without rejecting freedom. We can gradually make ourselves slaves to circumstance, and hand over our destiny to a world that often does not seem to care very much what it does with it.

As an alternative, we can punish ourselves. Some people go so far as to do this physically, sometimes causing themselves bodily pain and harm, sometimes fasting or depriving themselves of some pleasure. More often, we try to use regret and guilt as a kind of counterweight, somehow presuming that if we feel miserable enough, that will balance the scales.

None of these responses is what the Lord is looking for. Ezekiel perhaps said it best— "Have I any pleasure at all that the wicked should die? saith the Lord God: and not that he should return from his ways, and live?" If we recognize that we have done harm, then clearly the sanest response is to try to do well. It is to face the situation squarely, taking our misdeed simply as a fact to be reckoned with, and try to figure out what we can do about it.

"Charity," says Swedenborg, "is acting with prudence, to the end that good may result." Here is the situation; what can I do or say that has the best prospect of making things better?

One of the greatest obstacles to this attitude is a very common but very distorted image of God. It is the image of God as the strict father, the disciplinarian, who takes note of everything wrong and effects an appropriate punishment. This is an image we can find in Scripture on page after page; but it is what Swedenborgian theology refers to as "an appearance of truth." It is how we see the Lord when we ourselves are caught up in anger or guilt or self-righteousness. It may be the only image of God that will get through to us when we are in such states, and it is frequent in the Bible because it can be useful at such times.

Its use is limited, though, to preventing the worst. We may not follow our more destructive impulses because we fear the consequences. However, this kind of vengeful God will not inspire us to care for each other. The image deters us from evil rather than leads us to good.

There are other images of the Lord in the Bible that serve this latter purpose. Isaiah spoke to a nation suffering for its transgressions and said, "As one whom his mother comforts, so will I comfort you." Jesus looked at the city that was rejecting him, and said, "How often would I have gathered your children together, even as a hen gathers her chickens under her wings."

It is no coincidence that both of these are maternal rather than paternal images. Especially in an era when masculine strength is equated with hardness of heart, an exclusively masculine image of God is indeed a forbidding one. We need the gentler notes—the shepherd carrying lambs, the healer binding up wounds, the comforter, and often in our own world the most vivid experiences of this are the times when we have been hurt and have turned to mother's comfort and reassurance.

This, too, is what repentance is all about. When we have transgressed, we have hurt ourselves as well as others. In fact, since others have freedom to respond constructively to our wrongs, only the hurt to ourselves is inevitable. When we deny our transgression, we deny our hurt. When we punish ourselves, we add more hurt. Only when we acknowledge what we have done and turn to the Lord for comfort and healing are we acting realistically.

Think of this for a moment from the point of view of parents who care about their children. Think of the child who has gotten into trouble, and who refuses to admit it. The parents feel the pain of wanting to help, but being blocked by the denial. They do everything they can to make it easier for the child to acknowledge the misdeed, not in order to design punishment or to make the child feel guilty, but in order to get the matter out into the open where it can be dealt with.

Think of the doctor, if you will, and of the patient who comes only after the symptoms have become too painful to bear. "If only"—if only that patient had admitted that something was wrong when the first indications came, then the healing would have been far simpler and more complete.

We do need an image of God as gentle, loving, healing. It is not the only image we need, for in our more rebellious moods we would abuse that tolerance. But we need it often, and especially when the task of the moment is the task of repentance. We need to know that the Lord takes no pleasure in our pain, that the Lord is not saying, "You brought it on yourself." The Lord is saying, "What can we do about it? How can I make it better?"

There is another aspect to this that might be worth mentioning before closing. A major problem with the "punishment" view is that it misunderstands the nature of evil. The Lord does not add punishment to evil because evil is against his laws; evil is "against the Lord's laws" because it hurts. To believe that the Lord inflicts punishment for evils is to believe that the evils themselves do not hurt. If the Lord has to inflict pain in order to deter us from evil, then the assumption is that evil itself is pleasant.

"No good thing does he withhold from them that walk uprightly," said the Psalmist. The Lord does not forbid anything that would truly benefit us. Look at the people you know who are most at peace with themselves and with

145

their world, and you will not find any who are out to get all they can. You will find considerate, thoughtful individuals, people who are willing to go out of their way for you. Look at the most discontented people you know, and you will not find any thoughtful ones. Which is cause, and which is effect? Does contentment cause thoughtfulness, or does thoughtfulness cause contentment? It had better be the latter, for we are far more able to choose to be thoughtful than to choose to be contented.

We may rest assured that it is that latter. We may also take special note that thoughtfulness is developed particularly in times of difficulty. It is when we realize that we have been thoughtless that we face pivotal choices. We can take refuge in denial or self-justification or self-punishment, or we can respond thoughtfully. We can ask the same question that the Lord is asking— "What can I do that will make things better?"

"If ye love them which love you, what reward have ye? Do not even the publicans the same?" We are not much changed by being thoughtful when we feel like it, when everything is going well. The leverage for change is in our following this resolve when things have gone wrong.

We can do this consistently, I believe, only as we come to believe that the Lord is on our side in this effort. To the extent that we suspect that the Lord is out to requite evil for evil, we simply will not have confidence in the ultimate strength of our gentler impulses. We will be afraid that they are weak, and will have an inner feeling that real power lies in punishment and vengefulness. Repentance is full repentance only when it is turning to the gentle Lord, whose paternal truth is one with maternal care.

The Kingdom Forever

We have probably said the Lord's Prayer more times during our lives than we have said any other set of words. I suspect that different parts of it have had special meaning for us at different times. I suspect that at times it has been hard to focus on the meaning at all. But the practice is deeply ingrained, and the words are completely familiar.

I should like to focus on the closing statement of the prayer—in a sense on the closing word. It may seem at first glance as though this closing statement is out of place, since it does not ask for anything at all. "For thine is the kingdom and the power and the glory forever." (Matthew 6:13). It does not occur in Luke's version of the prayer, which is the one normally used in Catholic liturgy. Still, it seems appropriate to close the prayer with this kind of ascription, with this kind of recognition of the Father's eternal supremacy.

In fact, if we look a little more deeply at the rest of the prayer, we find that a similar kind of recognition is basic throughout. The most distinctive thing about the Lord's Prayer, I would suggest, is that it asks only for what is already the Lord's will. It is not a prayer to change the divine mind. Once we have asked that the holiness of the Lord's name be recognized, that the Lord's kingdom come and that his will be done, we have expressed the major theme. It is the divine intent that these things happen. It is also the divine intent to feed us daily, to forgive us, not to lead us into temptation, and to deliver us from evil. If any of these things are not happening, it is because we are somehow standing in the way. If the prayer is not "answered," it is we who need to change.

Under the surface appearance of a set of requests, then, the prayer is a description of the Lord's will for us. It is certainly appropriate to close that description with a recognition of the Lord's omnipotence. Clearly, all power and all glory are the Lord's, now and forever. Clearly, this is the most basic fact of our lives, the one thing above all that we need to know.

But what does it mean to say that the Lord's kingdom is forever? It would be easier if it said kingship, but it doesn't. This is the same kingdom whose coming is asked for at the outset of the prayer. We seem to be talking about something that has not yet happened, but that already is forever.

The problem goes back into the Old Testament, especially to the promise to David: "He shall build an house for my name, and I will stablish the throne of his kingdom for ever. . . . And thine house and thy kingdom shall be established for ever before thee: thy throne shall be established for ever."

Literally, of course, this did not happen. The dynasty of David did last for more than four centuries, which is quite extraordinary, but eventually it came to an end. The last actual king of the line died in captivity in Babylon; and when some of the people returned to rebuild Jerusalem and re-establish the nation, there was no effort (at least none is recorded) to set up a monarchy or to find out who the proper descendant of David would be.

In a slightly broader sense, though, the promise stayed alive. The hope that a descendant of David would emerge to restore the nation to its lost glory is clearly evident in the Gospels. When Jesus rode into Jerusalem on Palm Sunday, the crowds shouted "Hosanna to the son of David!" In fact, the Judaism of our own time has not forgotten that the destiny of the people is bound up with the coming of the Messiah. This is a "meantime" we are living in, between the destruction of the kingdom and the temple and their restoration.

When the Lord laid claim to the Messianic promises, though, he shifted their meaning significantly. He no longer talked about the kingdom of Israel. He talked instead about the kingdom of heaven or the kingdom of God. In his confrontation with Pilate, he made the explicit statement that his kingdom was not of this world.

This fits with the closing statement of the Lord's Prayer and points us toward a fuller understanding of it. It fits because nothing in this world is forever, and it points the way because it demands that we look then toward the spiritual world. After all, the prayer has already told us that the Lord's kingdom "is in heaven." It does not have to come there.

Now one of the more distinctive thoughts in Swedenborgian theology is that heaven is not just something that we hope will happen to us after we die. Heaven, like hell, is part of our present spiritual environment, and we are now making choices that move us toward it or away from it. "Everyone," wrote Swedenborg, "is born for heaven; and they are accepted into heaven who accept heaven into themselves in this world." The kingdom is trying to come to us here on earth.

We know quite a bit about this kingdom. Perhaps the most important thing we know is that it is a kingdom of mutual understanding and love expressed in action. We know this well enough that we have an acute sense of distress when we know we have fallen short. We know it well enough to rejoice at those times when its qualities are present and manifest in and around us.

This is not to say that there are no gray areas. There are many; and perhaps most of the time we are not entirely sure of ourselves. Certainly, we would rarely claim to have done the perfect deed or said the perfect sentence or made the perfect choice. It often seems that none of the options available to us is particularly heavenly, and we find ourselves trying to figure out which will do the least harm. But the fact remains that we do have a strong sense of what is good and what is not, strong enough that when no good alternative presents itself, we know it.

One of the clearer criteria we turn to in difficult times is that of duration. We are willing to endure, or even to inflict, a surprising amount of short-term pain if we are reasonably confident that the long-term results will be beneficial. In the immediate present, it hurts more to pull out a splinter than to leave it alone. The prospect of less pain over a longer period of time, and the risk of infection, send us looking for the tweezers. Correspondingly, we look at a promised pleasure and ask how long it will last, and if we believe it will be only fleeting, we do not attach much importance to it. We could imagine a kind of mathematical equation, in which we multiplied the intensity of the pleasure or pain by its duration in order to come up with an index of its importance to us.

If we were to do so, then the obvious winners, the most important aspects of our lives, would be those that were multiplied by "forever." In fact, the intensity would not matter at all, since even an intense pleasure over a period of years would not equal the slightest one lasting to eternity. Eventually, the little one would catch up.

There have been people who understood this in a way Swedenborgian theology would tend to disallow. These would be the people who chose to "mortify the flesh" in one way or another, in order to gain heavenly happiness after death. We could expand this category to include fanatics of every stripe, whose gaze is so fixed on some supposedly supreme value that they are heedless of the hurt they are giving here and now.

Such attitudes run counter to Swedenborgian theology because of our belief that heaven is beginning here and now. It is not a reward after death for misery in this life. It is not a compensation for having been cheated, or a payment for services rendered. It is an intrinsically fulfilling way of living together, a way that works here and now, not just after death. People who are accepting heaven into themselves are people at peace with themselves and with others. They know a basic contentment that carries them through all kinds of difficulties. They have hold of something solid that is immensely reassuring in this transitory world.

We need some touch of "forever" in our lives. We need

some constants—otherwise the change makes no sense whatever. As a kind of illustration, about every seven years, every cell in our body has been replaced. We have not become "different people," though, because there has been a constant through all this change. Otherwise, there would be no way to tell who we were, no basis for any sense of identity.

We need some touch of forever in our lives, and nothing in this world lasts forever. We need to look deeper, to the non-material, and it may take us some time to realize this. We have all seen people trying to maintain their identity by striving to stay physically young. We have seen churches trying to maintain their identity by clinging to the same outward forms of dress or of worship. If we watch long enough, we see that these efforts inevitably fail. The physical world will not stand still.

"For thine is the kingdom . . . forever." "Seek ye first the kingdom of God, and his righteousness." "My kingdom is not of this world." We are not called to other-worldliness, but to the discovery and affirmation of the eternal in the present. In every situation, there are some issues that are ephemeral, some that we might label fairly durable, and some that are eternal. There is no question what the Lord's priorities are. We read in *Divine Providence* n. 46, "In everything that it does, the Lord's divine providence focuses on what is infinite and eternal." The Lord is constantly looking at what matters forever.

In simplest form, what matters forever is how we accept the Lord and each other into our lives. The marriage of love and wisdom is the kingdom of God, and it is constantly trying to find realization in our day-to-day dealings with each other. In its very highest form, that marriage is the Divine it-self; and we, believe it or not, are created in that image and after that likeness. When we have moments of genuine self-forgetfulness, moments of genuine oneness with each other, we are in touch with the kingdom that is forever.

The Son of God

*While he spoke, behold, a bright
cloud overshadowed them: and
behold a voice out of the cloud,
which said, This is my beloved Son,
in whom I am well pleased;
hear him.*

Matthew 17:5

Probably all of you have shared in the discomfort of being in a Protestant church and hearing Jesus referred to as "the Son of God." This calls to mind a simplistic kind of trinitarian image, making Jesus at best a kind of emissary and at worst a human sacrifice to an angry deity. We are so accustomed to regarding Jesus as "God with us," as the very Divine taking on our human form and nature, that it is hard for us to listen to language that we ourselves do not use.

It is not that simple. First of all, this is the language of the Gospels themselves. In the chapter preceding the above quote, we find the following familiar incident.

> When Jesus came into the coasts of Cesarea
> Philippi, he asked his disciples, saying, "Whom do
> men say that I, the Son of man, am?" And they said,
> "Some say that you are John the Baptist: some,
> Elias; and others, Heremias, or one of the proph-
> ets." He replied, "But whom do you say that I am?"
> And Simon Peter answered and said, "You are the
> Christ, the Son of the living God."
>
> And Jesus answered and said unto him, "Blessed
> are you, Simon Bar-jona: for flesh and blood have
> not revealed it unto you, but my Father who is in
> heaven."
>
> Matthew 16:13–18

That is, Jesus is presented as approving Peter's identification of him as the Son of God, and as further confirming it by referring to God as his "Father who is in heaven."

Our text in chapter 17 comes from Matthew's account
of the transfiguration, that extraordinary event on the
mountain when Peter, James, and John were granted a
glimpse of the Lord's spiritual nature. If ever there was a
time during his earthly life when the Divine showed
through, this was it; and it was the very voice of the divine
which identified Jesus as "my beloved Son, in whom I am
well pleased." If we add the many instances in which Jesus
talks about his Father or talks to his Father, then the Gospel warrant for "the Son of God" is strong indeed.

As is often if not always the case, the problem is not so
much in the language itself as in the way we understand it.
It goes without saying in Swedenborgian circles that the Old
Testament images of God as vengeful and capricious are

"appearances," that they represent not so much the actual divine nature as the way in which that nature is perceived. In a dim way, they do reflect the truth that divine love is utterly opposed to evil in any form whatever. This is truth accommodated to our states when we ourselves are rebellious.

In much the same way, the identification of Jesus as "the Son of God" is an appearance, and a far less misleading one than those descriptions of God as vengeful and capricious. It is a phrase that draws on relationships we do know to give us some idea of a relationship that we do not know.

We should not expect it to be easy to describe the relationship between the infinite divine and the finite human. To our minds, they are incommensurate, since "finite" and "infinite" are opposites. We find Jesus, however extraordinary his powers, limited by both time and space. He walked from place to place. There were times when he was absent from his disciples. He lived for a limited time, and died. In Swedenborgian—and mainline Christian—terms, he was fully human. He does not seem much like the God who lays the beams of his chambers in the waters and makes the clouds his chariot, who walks on the wings of the wind, who laid the foundations of the earth and covered it with the deep as with a garment. Perhaps the simplest form the problem takes is in the question many of us have faced—"Who was running the universe while God was on earth?"

As long as we are limited to a literalistic understanding of Biblical language, there is no satisfactory answer to this question. To what Swedenborg would call "the natural mind," we are wholly discrete individuals. There is no question where I leave off and you begin. We cannot be in two places at once.

As we begin to wake up spiritually, though, we become conscious of a different set of rules. We discover that in countless ways we carry each other around inside us. Throughout our lives, we hear the voices of our parents and teachers. We accept thoughts from each other to the point where it is impossible to tell what is ours and what is others' in us. We pray without regard to time or place or direction, without worrying whether someone else is trying to get through to God at the same time. If we find it easier to pray in a particular place or in a particular posture, we realize that this is a kind of artificial help, a concession to our own limited abilities. In other words, we assume that God is capable of granting us undivided attention at any moment; and we seem to have evidence that this is indeed the case.

In fact, this is a central message of the first chapter of Swedenborg's *Divine Love and Wisdom* n. 78:

> It does seem as though the Divine were not the same in one person as in another—that it were different, for example, in a wise person than in a simple, different in an elderly person than in an infant. But this is the result of appearances, and is deceptive. The person is different, but the Divine is not different within the person. The person is a recipient, and the recipient or receptacle will vary.

Or in the words of *Apocalypse Revealed* n. 21, "The Divine is one and indivisible." The Divine cannot be less than totally present everywhere.

This means that when we speak of the Divine being totally present in Jesus, we are not talking about some exception to the rules. We are talking about a time when, contrary to the general run of appearances, the inner rules show through. God is just as totally present in each one of us as in the incarnation. The difference is in our receptivity, or more accurately, our acceptance. Just as it seems quite appropriate to think of ourselves as "children of God," the Gospel phrase "the Son of God" can be taken as an effort to express the fact that there is a difference between the actuality and the appearance.

The hard fact of the matter is that we do not want to accept more than a fraction of the Divine that is offered to us. We would like the light and strength to handle our own limited responsibilities. We are not particularly attracted by the prospect of having care for the salvation of the whole human race, of being filled with an intense and ceaseless love for every individual, anywhere, anytime.

This was borne in on me by contrast in reading a book on Buddhism.* The Bodhisattva is the individual who refuses simply to dwell in enlightenment as long as there remains one human being who has not attained it. The ideal was concisely expressed in this vow:

> I take upon myself the burden of all suffering.
> I am determined to bear it.
> I shall not turn back.
> I shall not flee or tremble.
> I shall not yield or hesitate.
> Why? Because the liberation of all beings is
> my vow.

---

* Lama Anagarika Govinda, *A Living Buddhism for the West* (Boston: Shambala, 1990), p. 93.

Buddhism is unusual among world religions in that formally it neither affirms nor denies the existence of God. What it does instead is assert quite uncompromisingly the absolute demand of particular qualities of heart and mind and life—the qualities of love, wisdom, and service. If we recall that for Swedenborg the "name" stands for the quality, the kinship is truly profound. The words of the Bodhisattva's vow would not be at all out of place in Jesus' mouth, and that is precisely the difference between Jesus and us.

We too believe that love and wisdom and service are the ultimate good of life. We express this by saying that love and wisdom and service are the Divine, are God. We recognize that we are called to reflect these qualities in our lives; but unlike the Bodhisattva, and unlike the incarnate Lord, we are content to ask only for the measure we feel we need for our own limited purposes.

This seems to represent a real difference in degree, but not a difference in kind. It may in fact be that we strive for the ideal "intensively," while the Buddhist strives "extensively." That is, we feel inadequate to deal with global problems until we can handle things on our more familiar small scale. The Buddhist feels inadequate to handle the individual relationship as long as compassion is limited to that scale. We are probably both right.

If we follow Swedenborgian theology faithfully, we do not worship the Jesus of the Gospels. We worship the risen and glorified Christ, and see in the incarnation a process which is the model for our own lives. Specifically in regard to our theme, the title "Son of God" might serve not so much to differentiate Jesus from us as to highlight this cen-

160

tral kinship. Jesus is not God in the sense of one who dwells on high and oversees the universe from a distance. In Jesus we see the Divine working as it works in our own lives, with everyday material. It is only in the glorified Christ that we see the complete union of the divine and the human which is the inevitable result of complete acceptance.

But again—and this cannot be stressed too strongly— the central issue is the issue of quality. We are called to love each other and to understand each other and to serve each other. If Buddhism does not give these qualities the name of "God," it nevertheless divinizes them by making them absolute and eternal necessities for fully human life. We, I believe, recognize that divinity more clearly, but run the risk of placing the qualities "out there somewhere" and divorcing them from our own lives.

We might do well, then, to listen again to the title, "the Son of God," hearing in it not a description of a separate individual, but an expression of the universal human state. For we, too, are creatures in whom the Divine is wholly present; and nothing but the fullest acceptance we can manage will make our lives worthwhile.

For Zion's Sake

I f we can identify at all with the prophet Isaiah, this is a potent enough passage simply in its literal meaning. There was a profound meaning to the city of Jerusalem. It had been the symbol of the vision realized, the center of all the hopes of Israel. The city and the temple had been the visible proof of God's care for them. They had been slaves in Egypt. They had been miraculously delivered and brought to this land. They had found independence and security, at least for a time. Not long before the time of our text, the temple had stood for almost four hundred years, through thick and thin—nearly twice as long as our own nation has existed.

But the closing chapters of Isaiah speak of a different time. They speak of a time when the unthinkable had happened, when Jerusalem and the temple had been destroyed. All the old certainties were shattered, all the old foundations were gone. Nothing made sense any more.

There was a milder parallel in our own century which may help us understand in some measure. At the beginning of the century, there was an extraordinary optimism. America stood on the threshold of the millennium, at the door to perfect peace and plenty. Scientific progress was stunning and would soon solve any remaining problems. It was Christianity that was nurturing this progress, and the success of this nation proved beyond doubt the supremacy of that religion. It was only a question of time before Christianity and the peace and plenty of science would sweep over the whole globe. We were the "light to the nations."

The terrible destruction of the First World War raised doubts, but it was still possible to see this as the final conflict, as the war "to make the world safe for democracy." The Second World War, though, with the specters of genocide in both Europe and the Far East, destroyed that optimism; and the immense cloud of the nuclear threat remains, along with profoundly alarming social symptoms, to inhibit any rebirth.

In mood, then, Isaiah's times were not all that different from our own; and for me at least, this makes his message all the more striking. "For Zion's sake I will not hold my peace, and for Jerusalem's sake I will not rest, until the righteousness thereof goes forth as brightness, and the salvation thereof as a burning lamp." It seems as though the vision shone all the more brightly in contrast to the utterly disheartening circumstances. Jerusalem never had been heaven on earth, but it had been possible to pretend that it was. Now it was no longer possible to pretend, to substitute the actual for the ideal, so now the ideal stood forth in full clarity.

This has its literal relevance to our own lives. It is stated about as concisely as possible in *Proverbs*: "Where there is no vision, the people perish." There is a significant difference between resisting what we see as wrong and working for what we see as right, between trying to avert the worst and trying to achieve the best. When we are trying only to avert the worst, we tend to see only the problems and not the resources. We slip unconsciously into regarding other people as problems, and address them as needing to change. We become the constant critics, always expecting the worst; and when this is our attitude, we actually intend to elicit the worst. Others find it necessary to be on their guard with us and find it hard not to act as adversaries.

Given an affirmative vision of what might be, though, this changes. We begin to address each other as potential companions, alert to every hint of good intent. We begin to notice the good things, to call the attention of others to them, to encourage them and build on them. We begin to expect better, if not the best, and when this is our attitude, this is what we tend to elicit. Others discover that they can trust us to understand and appreciate them. There is no need to act as adversaries, even when there is disagreement. There is every reason to share.

We are talking about two kinds of circles. The negative outlook elicits negative responses, which confirm the negativity. The affirmative vision elicits affirmative responses, which confirm the vision. As we see what the vision can do from day to day, on a small scale, we become more and more convinced of its worth. We come to realize that it is intrinsically valid, even though it may not work every time.

This, I suspect, is the core value of "positive thinking," and it is worth noting that it can be abused. We are not talking about rose-colored glasses or about closing our eyes to what is wrong within and around us. We are talking about a realistic awareness that the "wrong" is not the whole story, and about a constant sensitivity to what is right within and around us.

We may well wonder whether Isaiah had reached that point. Shortly after the destruction of Jerusalem, there was not much in his circumstances to strengthen the vision. This, in a sense, is where theology and worship come in. As Swedenborgian theology tells us, our minds do have the capacity to rise above our circumstances and to glimpse what might be. That vision in and of itself can be so convincing that we take it with us when we go back down to the level of our everyday involvements. There is a brightness to the righteousness. The vision is like a burning lamp. It does entail a longing to share it, a restlessness, and an unwillingness to hold our peace.

It is a very short step from here to the spiritual sense of our text, because Zion represents "the celestial of faith" or "the celestial church." This is the church, as an individual or as a community, where love actually reigns. In more down-to-earth terms, it is the church we glimpse in fact when we are at our best, when we are moved to a genuine appreciation of each other and care for each other, when from that care we give our fullest energies to understanding clearly and to speaking and acting well.

This may stand out more clearly by contrast. The "natural church" would take things more or less at face value, with primary attention to what was being done. It would feed the hungry and minister to the sick because these are good things to do in the face of obvious problems. The "spiritual church" would try to understand what we might call the horizontal causes of hunger and sickness, and in dealing with this, it would tend to "go by the book." That

166

is, it would focus on teaching, on seeing clearly what was going on. The "celestial church" would see the hunger and sickness as symptoms of a deeper distress, and would be spontaneously sensitive to "the heart of the matter." All three would give food and physical care. The spiritual would add teaching to these, and the celestial would further add the gift of self.

By themselves, the natural and the spiritual are necessary but not sufficient. They deal with problems that must be dealt with, but they do not address the roots of those problems. There will continue to be inequity just as long as we remain insensitive to each other, just as long as our consciousness is dominated by awareness of ourselves. As caring gains strength within us, though, we find ourselves incapable of being contented in the presence of distress. We find the vision calling us more and more constantly. We find ourselves urged on by every experience of the gap between what is and what might be.

In a way, this requires not so much the development of a new sensitivity as attention to sensitivities we already have. By way of illustration, the generation that reacted to the Second World War was not "more empathetic" than we are. Like us, they were affected by the mood or the spirit of the times. We ourselves find it hard to remain optimistic when the news is grim day after day, hard not to feel hopeful when, for example, the Iron Curtain begins to part, and the military threat seems to recede.

On a more intimate level, while we rarely have direct experiences of the feelings of others, we do pick up and respond to very subtle physical indications; and I suspect that if we had the means of determining it, we would find that we are also picking up indications on a non-physical level. We are not closed individual systems, but integral aspects of community, culture, and world—in the words of one writer, "relatively autonomous sub-totalities." In our own unique ways, we all reflect and in a way summarize the world (or worlds) we live in. We are not so much parts of a machine as participants in a body, constantly giving and receiving.

Swedenborg's *Heaven and Hell* offers us a vision of what that "body" can become. It is not so much a book about what is going to happen after we die as a description of what life is all about here and now, because our eternal life has already begun. It is saying, in a sense, that there are constant potentials for "heavenly moments" within us, between us, and among us, and that our task is not to create such moments, but to recognize and accept them when they are offered. The people who are accepted into heaven are the ones who have accepted heaven into themselves in this world.

Such moments rarely reach out and grab us, and it would be idle to pretend that they are always within easy reach. There are times when the ideal seems impossibly remote, times we have come to call "depression." About all we can do in such times is hang on, learn whatever we can, and remind ourselves that eventually things will change. Much of the time, though, we are in a kind of balance and are offered the opportunity to tip the scales. There is a moment of truer humanity available, but we will not see it unless we are looking for it.

The vision helps us to be attentive, and our attentiveness strengthens and clarifies the vision. As we see more and more clearly how sane and how beautiful is the Lord's will for us, individually and collectively, Isaiah's words become our own: For Zion's sake I will not hold my peace, and for Jerusalem's sake I will not rest, until the righteousness thereof goes forth as brightness, and the salvation thereof as a burning lamp.

The Bonds of Society

The radical change in Soviet policies under Gorbachev has raised hopes for world peace to a level they have not reached since the nuclear arms race began. In many ways, the change of climate is refreshing, and I would not want to cast a cloud over it; but at the same time, I believe that if we look at our world in the light of Swedenborgian theology, we cannot escape the conclusion that we have still a long way to go. We are making progress, I would insist, but the millennium is not just around the corner. When our own Pentagon defines peace as "permanent pre-hostility," we seem to have a problem right here at home.

We might start, then, by looking at what we mean by peace. The desire for peace finds one of its most conspicuous forms in efforts toward disarmament, and especially toward the abolition of nuclear weapons. The end of war, however, is not the same as the achievement of peace. A nuclear holocaust would bring an and to war. Let me quote from *Arcana Coelestia* n. 5662 (2):

> At this day scarcely anyone knows what is the
> "peace" which is mentioned in the Word; as in the

benediction. . . . Almost everyone believes that peace is security from enemies, and that it is tranquility at home, and among our companions; but this peace is not meant there, but a peace which immeasurably transcends that peace. It is heavenly peace. . . . No one can be gifted with this peace, except one who is led by the Lord, and is in the Lord, that is, in heaven, where the Lord is the all in all. For heavenly peace inflows when the cupidities which originate from the love of self and of the world have been taken away; for these are the things which take away peace, for they infest the interiors of man, and cause him at last to place rest in unrest, and peace in things which cause troubles; because [they cause him to place] delight in evils. So long as man is in these, he cannot possibly know what peace is; nor even so long as he believes that this peace is of no account.

The next thing that must be said is that heavenly peace is an active state. Again from *Arcana Coelestia* n. 454:

Some suppose that heaven consists in an idle life, in which they are served by others. But they are told that no happiness ever consists in being at rest, and thence having happiness; for thus everyone would want to have the happiness of others for himself; and when everyone wanted this, no one would have it. Such a life would not be active, but idle, in which they would become torpid. . . . The angelic life consists in use . . . .

This last statement, "the angelic life consists in use," brings us straight to the statement from which my title is taken. It is from *Marriage Love* n. 18 and reads as follows:

> No one is wise, or lives, for himself alone. . . . To live for others is to do uses. Uses are the bonds of society, which are as many in number as there are good uses; and uses are infinite in number.

"Uses are the bonds of society." The implications of this simple statement are extensive. Put together with the previous quotations, it is saying that peace is something we must do. It is not just a nice feeling, not the knowledge that no one wants to hurt us or that we are strong or isolated enough to be safe. Peace is an active and constructive way of living together; and since it is inseparable from use, we can experience it on any scale, simply by focusing on our own use in whatever situation we find ourselves.

Let me give a simple and general example. It can be disturbing to be misunderstood. Say we have tried to do something worthwhile, and others see this as aggressive behavior, as an effort to butt in or to put them down. As long as we focus on our own wounded ego, on the injustice we are suffering, we are disturbed. But suppose we find the wisdom to look at our use in this situation. Suppose, that is, we start trying to see what we can do that will actually make things better. Our whole mood changes. We experience the kind of peace that comes when we are totally absorbed in doing something we love to do.

"Uses are the bonds of society." This, I would suggest, is Swedenborg's answer to the Jacques Brel song that was popular some time ago, "If We Only Have Love." To quote Swedenborg again:

> Love and wisdom, without use, are not anything, but are only ideal entities, and do not become real until they are in use; for love, wisdom, and use are three things which cannot be separated; if separated, neither of them is anything.
>
> *Apocalypse Revealed* n. 875

It is far too easy to get caught up in self-analysis, berating ourselves with the thought that we should not be feeling the way we do. We try in vain to make ourselves feel differently, to suppress the resentment or the anger, but this is simply not effective. What we can do much more usefully is to shift our attention away from ourselves at such times. OK, the anger and resentment are there. I may not be able to banish them by an effort of will, but they do not need to control my behavior. Is there anything I can do or say that will help? It may even be expressing the negative feelings— that is by no means ruled out. It may very well be saying out loud, "That hurts," not to defend or justify ourselves, but to help nurture mutual understanding. If it succeeds, we are delighted, and if it fails, then we try something else. The main point is that we find ourselves operating from a place within ourselves that is not threatened, from a place of peace. We find that place by focusing on the use that can be found in the particular moment. "Love and wisdom, without use, are not anything, but are only ideal entities, and do not become real until they are in use . . . ."

I think it is clear, on this scale, how inevitably and effectively "uses are the bonds of society." All we have to do is to imagine a community in which this was the dominant spirit, in which every problem that arose prompted people to look for the most helpful way to deal with it. It would be an extraordinarily close and peaceful community, and at the same time a thoroughly active one. Further, this kind of peace would be wonderfully resilient, because it would not depend on everything going right all the time. It would not be destroyed by outbreaks of anger or even of violence. Such incidents would instead call forth extra efforts, would call forth the very best the community could muster.

I once read a newspaper article about a woman in the Midwest who styled herself as an expert in writing effective letters of complaint, and who could back this up with results. Her first rule, as I remember it, was to assume that the person she was complaining to was not the individual who had made the mistake. As a result, her letters were never angry or self-righteous. She focused on clarity, and wrote with the assumption that the company wanted to do things right. I would recommend her as an example of a genuine peacemaker, and stress the fact that she was not making peace by abdicating her own rights or by ignoring wrongs. If this were the prevalent attitude, we would have not only a "kinder and gentler" America, but a more just one as well.

There is abundant evidence, however, that this is not the prevalent attitude. After a brief affair with idealism during the Kennedy years, we seem as a nation to have fallen hopelessly in love with money, for its own sake. Polls taken of high school seniors show the principal goal in life as "making lots of money"—a sharp and apparently dismaying shift from the years in which the Peace Corps was attracting young people by the thousands. College graduates are flocking in unprecedented numbers to Wall Street, and our headlines are full of stories of people making fortunes by the manipulation of money. When a company can come away from a failed takeover with a profit of millions of dollars, when a company is ripe for takeover because it is investing seriously in research instead of turning a quick profit, the foundations of our economy are shaky indeed. When the hero of the hour is the entrepreneur rather than the statesman or the healer or the discoverer, then the focus is not on use.

This is not a question of one political party as against another. It is a question of our national mood and of our national priorities. We will begin to see world peace, I would suggest, when we begin to ask out loud what use our nation can be to the rest of the world. Whatever the theorists may claim, competition motivated by greed will not usher in universal prosperity, and neither will the redistribution of wealth. We will have an economy of scarcity just as long as the name of the game is to contribute the minimum and extract the maximum. We will begin to experience surpluses when we look first of all to our contribution, our use, and draw out only what we need to perform that use. Or as it is stated in Swedenborgian theology:

> Good uses are, to provide for one's self and one's
> own the necessaries of life; to desire an abundance
> for the sake of one's country, and the neighbor,
> whom a rich man can in many ways benefit more
> than a poor man; and also because he can in this
> way remove his disposition from an idle life, which

is pernicious, for in it a man thinks evilly, from the
evil implanted in him.

Heaven and Hell n. 361

It is becoming abundantly clear that the poor and the
oppressed are not somehow automatically virtuous. On the
individual level, when abused children attain adult strength,
they very often become abusive parents. On the national
scale, revolutions by violence most often seem to produce
new tyrannies, as we are beginning to recognize especially
in the former colonies in Africa. Before women were
granted the right to vote in this country, as astute an individual as Helen Keller honestly believed that once women
could vote, there would be no more war. In Israel, we are
seeing perhaps the most oppressed people of the world
discovering the pitfalls of power. It is not, I would suggest,
that "power corrupts, and absolute power corrupts absolutely." It is that power enables us to do what we wish, and
strips the masks off from our selfishness.

What would it be like to "desire an abundance for the
sake of one's country and the neighbor"? It would be to
have a mission in life, a contribution that one wanted
deeply to make, and to work fairly and honestly for the
resources to make that contribution. Or let me make another, perhaps less palatable, suggestion. It would be to
avoid the lottery because one might win, and thereby be
faced with the responsibility of contributing something of
at least equal value.

The relevance of this may be clearer in the light of another quotation, bearing in mind the general principle that uses are the bonds of society.

> By uses are meant not only the necessaries of life
> . . . for one's self and one's own; but also the good
> of our country, of the community, and of our fel-
> low-citizen. Mercantile business is such a good
> when the love of it is the end, and money is a me-
> diate subservient love; provided the man of busi-
> ness shuns and is averse to defraudings and evil
> arts as sins.
>
> *Divine Providence* n. 220 (11)

The flow of goods and services is a primary factor in the unity of our country. We have prospered relative to the rest of the world in large measure because of the scale on which we could operate, the area, resources, and population included within our boundaries, without barriers to commerce. We are currently looking with some anxiety at the nascent European Common Market, which could provide stiff competition in spite of its linguistic diversity. We have long been aware that either Russia or China could dominate economically if either could resolve its own internal problems.

We should also be aware that international trade can be one of the most potent forces for world unity, provided there is mutual benefit. The more clearly both parties profit from an arrangement, the more remote is the likelihood of war between them. By the same token, when the benefit is one-sided, the effect is divisive. When a country's personal and natural resources are exploited, as was often the case under colonialism and is still characteristic of too many third-world countries, then it may seem to the exploited that they have nothing to lose and everything to gain by armed insurrection.

If it seems overly idealistic to expect international conglomerates to renounce any form of exploitation or inequity, that is simply an indication of how far we have to go before we are within reach of world unity. Try telling the head of a major company that "Mercantile business is such a good when the love of it is the end, and money is a mediate subservient love," and see how far you get. We could make significant steps toward world peace if our legal structures rewarded companies for the equity of their dealings. We could make some steps toward world peace if such companies got impartial publicity, and there were equally impartial reporting of abuses; but the direct effects of legal encouragement would be more effective.

The principle is the same as the personal one, focusing first on the contribution we can make, and regarding the profit to ourselves simply as a means to that contribution. We cannot honestly recommend to others policies that we are unwilling to adopt for ourselves; but there is more to it than that. We cannot add up a vast number of small, personal inequities and expect the sum to be fairness and justice. The Gospels tell us that those who are faithful in little things are faithful also in great things. And Swedenborgian theology puts this principle more philosophically, as follows:

> For every general use is composed of innumerable ones, which are called mediate, administering, and

> subservient uses. All and each are coordinated and
> subordinated according to Divine order, and, taken
> together, they constitute and perfect the general
> use, which is the common good.
>
> *Heaven and Hell* n. 392

Ronald Reagan did not so much change the mood of the country as strengthen what was already there by giving it voice. So did Washington, Lincoln, Grant, Hoover, and all the rest, some for better and some for worse. Just as our single votes are essential to the working of a democratic system, no matter how insignificant they may seem, so our own attitudes are integral to the national mood. In fact, they are far more powerful than our votes, because they directly influence all the people we deal with. We contribute to a more peaceful country, to a kinder and gentler America, whenever we treat anyone kindly and gently, and the more consistent, the more persistent we are in our kindness and gentleness, the more contagious is our example.

This does not and cannot mean glossing over evils. To quote Swedenborg again:

> But man does not feel and perceive the love of
> doing uses for the sake of uses, as he does the love
> of doing uses for the sake of self; and therefore,
> while he is doing uses, he does not know whether
> he is doing them for the sake of the uses, or for the
> sake of self. But let him know that he is doing uses
> for the sake of uses in proportion as he is shunning
> evils; for in proportion as anyone is shunning

these, in the same proportion he is doing uses, not
from himself, but from the Lord.

Arcana Coelestia n. 3796

If our kindness and gentleness lead us to pretend that
nothing is wrong, then they are not from a love of use. They
are almost certainly from a desire to be liked, from a corresponding fear of offending. But on the principle that the
good in the neighbor is the neighbor to be loved, this desire and fear are wholly misleading. The good in the neighbor is not some abstract principle; it is the angel-to-be, the
Lord flowing in. When the focus is on use, then we address
the "erring neighbor" on the assumption that that individual
wants to do his or her best. We stand with that person
against his or her failings. "Shunning evils" cannot be restricted to our treatment of ourselves, if we are to love our
neighbor as we love ourselves.

This has its international equivalent, and I should like to
back up for a moment to ground the next point in a central
assertion of Swedenborgian theology. That assertion is that
all life flows in from the Lord. At the point at which it flows
in, it is utterly pure and heavenly, but that point, "the inmost,"
is quite beyond the reach of our consciousness. As the life
flows through the deeper levels of our being, it is first indi-
vidualized, and eventually distorted by the unregenerate
forms of our own inheritance and our own making.

If we trace this process in reverse, something interesting
happens. We find ourselves looking first at some of our more
antisocial tendencies, finding what may seem to be their
roots in our self-concern, and then discovering that this very

181

self-concern has deeper and more legitimate roots. The strength—as opposed to the form—of every desire we feel is the Lord's strength. There is a valid basis for every human effort, however destructive. The Lord is the life of the hells.

On the international scene, this suggests that whenever another nation is at cross purposes with us, we should first of all try to seek out the legitimate roots of both our and their efforts. There are two major benefits to this. First of all, as we discover what it is that we legitimately want, we can become more flexible in our means without in any way compromising our principles. Second, and equally important, we can begin to talk to the other nation in terms it can understand, because that nation sees its intentions as legitimate. It is heartening at this time in history, for example, to see other nations concerned about our national deficit spending. It may be that in the long run, the most beneficial result of the Reagan years will be the sharp rise in foreign investment in the American economy. We are no longer the world's banker, but are its greatest debtor. We have lost our economic independence, and that may well be just what the doctor ordered.

I want to close, though, by stressing the importance of our own individual focus on use. National policies simply cannot rise much higher than the general level of morality, no matter what the form of government; and in a democracy the tie is particularly close. I'd like to read, in this connection, a fascinating quote which at first hearing may seem a bit unrelated.

> All kinds of seeds are opened by warmth, right to their center. They are impregnated by the subtlest

substances, which can only come from a spiritual source, and thus empowered to yoke themselves to use. This results in their ability to reproduce, and then, in combination with elements of natural origin, to construct forms of uses. Then they bring these forth, as if from the womb, so that they reach the light, and so sprout and grow. Thereafter, the effort is unceasing from the earth through the roots to the extremities, and from the extremities to first things where the use exists in its source.

This is how uses cross over into forms. And forms derived from use, which is like a soul, as they proceed from first to final and from final back to first things, derive the characteristic that each and every detail is of some use. We say that the use is like a soul because its form is like a body.

It also follows that there is a more inward effort, the effort to bring forth uses through sprouting, for the sake of the animal kingdom; for animals of every kind are nourished by plants. It also follows that there is a most inward effort—the effort to be useful to the human race.

Divine Love and Wisdom n. 310

We can take this back a step, if we wish. We can look at a stone, which would seem to have no "prolific principle" whatever. But it holds soil in place, and very gradually disintegrates to form new soil. From this grow plants, which nourish animals, including people, who are potential angels. The great purpose of world peace is made up of countless little purposes. To quote again:

For every general use is composed of innumerable
ones, which are called mediate, administering, and
subservient uses. All and each are coordinated and
subordinated according to Divine order, and, taken
together, they constitute and perfect the general
use, which is the common good.

Heaven and Hell n. 392

"The common good," on the natural level, is nothing
less than world peace—peace, that is, regarded as living
together in the spirit of mutual care. The bonds of society
are formed or severed in our dealings with each other, because we are mediate, administering and subservient uses.
We strengthen the foundations of the common good by
some actions, and undermine them by others; and one final quote may serve to define our task, on whatever level
we may be called to serve:

The worship of the Lord itself consists in performing uses; and uses are [in this life] that everyone
should rightly discharge his function in his station;
thus [they consist in his] being of service to his
country, to societies, and to the neighbor, from the
heart; in his acting sincerely with his associates;
and in performing kind offices prudently, according to the quality of each person. These uses are
chiefly the exercises of charity; and are those
through which the Lord is chiefly worshipped. Fre-
quenting a place of worship, prayers, etc., are also
necessary; but without those uses, are of no avail;
for these things are not of life; but teach what the
life should be.

Arcana Coelestia n. 7038

In Search of Hierarchy

Mainstream Christian theology has for some time been focused on issues of social injustice. "Liberation theology" in general, with such subcategories as feminist theology and black theology, has raised urgent questions about the participation of Christian churches in a world of dismaying inequality, and about the role of theology as tending to reflect and justify the status quo. There has been a tendency to highlight those passages in both Old and New Testaments that criticize the rich and advocate the poor. One recent scholarly introduction to the Old Testament goes so far as to see the period of the Judges as Israel's golden age, when there was an egalitarian society and when social problems were taken care of by informal networks. The author then proceeds to label the monarchy as "Israel's counter-revolutionary establishment."

In the general schema, the basic problem is seen as one of unequal distribution of power. The poor, the minorities, or women, are seen as "marginalized" by their exclusion from circles of power. The solution is therefore to "empower" them. In the jargon of the trade, there are writers who insist on "a hermeneutics of suspicion" in the case of more traditional theologies, and claim "hermeneutical privilege" for the marginalized. In more colloquial terms, this means that one cannot take anything a traditional theologian says at face value, while what the minority theologian says is exempt from criticism.

On the intellectual level, this is a frontal assault on the problem, a direct effort to redress the imbalance. The minorities have not been heard. The "establishment theologians" have been heard too much. The goal seems again to be an egalitarian society; and in liberation theology circles, "hierarchy" is almost as derogatory a term as "patriarchal."

What does this have to do with creation spirituality? I want to argue that on this particular issue, on the issue of the distribution of power, creation spirituality and liberation theology tend to be diametrically opposed to each other. Creation spirituality is profoundly and thoroughly hierarchical. If one reads or listens to Matthew Fox, there are countless references to higher and lower values. A theology is not to be criticized because it is propounded by a white male, nor is it to be espoused because it is propounded by a black female. It is to be considered compassionately regardless of its source, in an effort to understand it first of all, and to see what it implies. If it has no underlying cosmology, it will not help us find our fitting place in the scheme of things. If it does not leave room for mystical experience, it will cut us off from a major source of spiritual light and strength.

And if Matthew Fox's theology is broadly hierarchical, Swedenborg's is hierarchical in detail. One can scarcely read a page without coming on some reference to higher and lower, or (which is the same thing) more or less internal. We read early and often about the celestial, spiritual, and natural heavens, arranged one above the other. But let me give you a sample quote:

> ... there are three heavens. The first is where good spirits live, the second is where angelic spirits live, and the third is where angels live. Their degrees of perfection are heightened the way more outward things relate to more inward ones. It is almost like the relationship between hearing and sight, and between sight and thought. That is, what hearing can take in in an hour can be presented visually in a minute—as, for example, a country landscape or a view of mansions or cities; and what the eye can see over a space of hours can be grasped by thought in a minute. This is like the ratio between the language of spirits and that of angelic spirits, and between the language of these latter and that of angels. In one concept of their language or thought, angelic spirits can actually grasp more than spirits can with some thousands; and there is a similar ratio between angels and angelic spirits.
>
> *Arcana Coelestia* n. 1642

Since Swedenborg is talking here about speech and language in heaven, he presents the intellectual side of this hierarchy—the concepts of higher angels are vastly more perfect than those of lower ones. But there is, of course, more to it than that. This is very definitely a hierarchy of power as well. I quote again, "... one angel is more powerful than tens of thousands of hellish spirits ... " (*Arcana Coelestia,* n. 3417).

But it is not just a matter of intellect and power. It is first and foremost a matter of love. *Heaven and Hell*, n. 479, begins with the statement that "After death, we are our own love, or our own intentionality." It continues:

> The whole of heaven is divided into communities on the basis of differences in the good of love [which I'll have more to say about shortly]. All the spirits who are transported to heaven and become angels are taken to the community where their love is, and on arrival are, so to speak, with themselves, as though they were in the house where they were born. . . . then whatever does not make one with their ruling love is put aside and apparently taken away. If they are good, then everything that is discordant or in disagreement is put aside and apparently taken away, and they are in this way brought into their own love. The same thing happens to evil people, with the difference that it is true things that are taken away from them, while it is false things that are taken away from the good.

This, I would suggest, brings us to the root of Swedenborg's hierarchical view of reality. It is summed up in *True Christian Religion*, n. 394f. The title of the section is "There are three universal loves—love of heaven, love of the world, and love of self." It continues (I abbreviate considerably):

> We begin with these three loves because they are the universal and fundamental [aspects] of everything. . . . By love of heaven we mean love of the Lord and also love of the neighbor. . . . Love of the world is not just love of wealth and possessions,

but love of everything the world provides, everything that delights the physical senses, as beauty delights the eyes, harmony the ears, fragrance the nostrils, delicacies the tongue, and caresses the skin. . . . Love of self is not just a love of honor, glory, renown and eminence, but also a love of earning and seeking positions of influence and thereby controlling other people. . . .

[395.] These three loves are in every one of us from creation and therefore from birth, and when they are properly subordinated, they perfect us as humans; and when they are not properly subordinated, they distort us.

The social message of this particular version is, I think, clear. The empowerment of the marginalized will not necessarily bring us any closer to a just society. The only change that can move us toward that goal is the empowerment of the compassionate. This can be accomplished either by identifying the compassionate and empowering them, or by finding those in power and converting them to compassion. Neither of these means is at all simple or easy, but there are instances of both. We know that they can happen because they have happened.

It seems unrealistic or idealistic to think that they can happen with enough regularity to make a major difference to our planet. In rebuttal, though, I would ask that we look honestly at what the "realists" have done. We have had successful revolutions against tyranny—empowerments of the disenfranchised. One of these happened about three-quarters of a century ago in Russia, and the extent of its disastrous consequences is just becoming evident. One of them happened much more recently, with the victory of the North Vietnamese. It led not to a just society but to genocide in Cambodia. Idi Amin was not more benevolent than his colonial predecessors, and in general the native governments in former African colonies have been oppressive and corrupt.

There is the rather cynical statement that "power corrupts, and absolute power corrupts absolutely." If it is true that power corrupts, then the equal empowerment of everyone would simply mean that we would all be equally corrupt. It would be more accurate, I am sure, to say that it is easy to be righteous when you are powerless to do anything bad on a scale big enough to attract attention. Power amplifies our intentions and broadcasts them. We give lip service to the Gospel principle that faithfulness or faithlessness in least things means faithfulness or faithlessness in great things, but we do tend to shy away from it when things get tough.

Let me take an example that could be closer to home. I trust we would agree that having power entails a corresponding responsibility. I trust we would also agree that having money grants us a corresponding amount of power. When we think of having more money—whether by writing a best-seller or getting a marvelous raise or winning the lottery—do we ask ourselves seriously whether we are ready for that responsibility? Do we look carefully at the way we are handling the responsibility we have now? This is not a frivolous question. One of Mike Tyson's trainers made the same point recently in a very concrete way. "If you take someone from reform school and give him four or five million dollars, what do you expect?"

In a way, we might say that the critical task is to break the apparent tie between power and control. What we know about ourselves and what we can observe around us tells us that the need to be in control is a sure sign of insecurity. It points to weakness rather than to strength. I'm reminded of the story of the time the minister left his sermon on the pulpit, and the custodian became intrigued by the marginal notes. After one paragraph was the underlined word, PAUSE. At the top of the next page were the words, "Lean forward, lower voice." And next to one paragraph he read, "Weak point: yell like hell!"

The last thought I should like to offer is that the effort to link power with compassion tends to bring concern for spiritual growth and concern for social action together, where I believe they belong. If spiritual growth is conceived of as a strictly private matter, as involving only an inner relationship to God, then it does lead to disengagement from the world around us. If social action is conceived of as strictly the redesign of societal machinery, then it becomes oblivious to the hearts from which both justice and injustice arise. The moment we take seriously the task of uniting compassion and power, though, we are brought face to face with our own exercise of power as well as with what we see around us. We very soon learn that the mote in our neighbor's eye cannot be divorced from the plank in our own, that if we are to show others "the way," we must walk in it ourselves. If we are to work effectively for a compassionate society, we must discover at first hand what compassion is.

As If

In a way, it should come as no surprise that the four Gospel accounts of the resurrection do not agree in detail. When something extraordinary happens, something that touches us to the heart, we are in no mood to take notes on the event for the sake of posterity. Our emotions are churning, and our minds are confused. We do not know what to make of things.

And it does indeed seem certain that something extraordinary happened. We must recall that the disciples had become deeply attached to Jesus. He had become the meaning of their lives and their hope for the future. Suddenly, just when it had seemed that he was moving toward triumph, utter disaster had struck. The matchless intimacy of the Last Supper had been followed by the unthinkable—the betrayal, the trial, the crucifixion, the death, the burial. Anyone who doubts the resurrection must explain what it was that so completely reversed the disciples' mood. What inspired them to go out into a hostile world with such complete conviction? What empowered them to preach and to heal? What enabled them to face death with such equanimity?

They had not figured out some intellectual explanation

of the events. That could have done no more than enable them to live with defeat. It could not have been one individual's private, inner experience which was then related to others. Paul had such an experience, and it seems that some of the disciples never did believe him. No, something happened to them all, something they did not really understand, but which was utterly and absolutely convincing.

We have no direct access to that experience itself. If Peter, who witnessed it, went away wondering what had happened, we can only read the accounts and wonder for ourselves. But as the events affected Peter because they touched issues central to his life, so the accounts can affect us as they touch issues central to ours; and that is what I want to talk about. Whatever may have changed over the centuries, we remain profoundly concerned with death and life.

Physical death is an absolute necessity. As the flowers and shrubs outdoors come to life again after their winter's dormancy, they are nourished by the decaying substance of previous generations. Our own bodies depend on plants and animals that were once alive. And perhaps more to the point, each generation of humans must give way to the next, must make room, if that next generation is to assume its full responsibility and maturity.

We live in confidence that physical death is not the end of the story. There is abundant evidence in Swedenborgian theology that our individuality is primarily spiritual rather than physical, and that the death of the body simply opens the door so that we begin living consciously the lives we are leading inwardly now.

On that level, we face the issues of life and death in a

different form. Most simply put, being truly alive spiritually is to be actively engaged with other people. It is to be emotionally sensitive to their needs, mentally alert to what is going on, and energetic in our efforts to be of use. Spiritual death is to become wrapped up in ourselves, grasping for whatever we want. It is to desensitize ourselves to the feelings and needs of others, to rationalize everything in our own favor, and to try to get the most from the world while contributing the least.

A central message of the Easter story—perhaps the central message, is precisely this, that spiritual life is self-giving. The Lord's life among us was his gift of himself. To anyone who would accept, he gave his love, his thought, his healing. Ultimately, he gave his physical life, with no effort to preserve it. Swedenborgian theology tells us that this is essentially why he rose from the dead. Love is the essence of life, and absolute love is absolute life.

We are not called to anything so dramatic, but we face the same issues every day. We are neither wholly loving nor wholly selfish; and we regularly find ourselves at odds with ourselves. There is something we want very much, perhaps something as simple as a few moments' peace and quiet, and there is a duty insisting on attention.

Often, I think, we make things difficult for ourselves by misperceiving the situation. We see "what we want" as originating wholly from our own desires, and we see the duty as wholly imposed from the outside. The choice becomes a choice between "us and them," and there is a legitimacy to our own needs. It may help to realize that this is only part of the truth. Yes, the duty arises from our circumstances, but the call to duty comes from within ourselves. The feelings of responsibility are our own. They are not imposed on us by others. And in similar fashion, there is an "outside" aspect to our need for peace and quiet. We are affected by the world around us, and sometimes it does get to us.

When we find ourselves in such situations, then, it is not simply a question of whether we serve ourselves or others. It is also a question of which part of ourselves we heed and nourish. Negatively, do we deny ourselves rest which we may need, or do we take on feelings of guilt? It seems clear that these are questions which no one else can answer for us.

It also seems clear that there is more involved than simply which choice we make. What perhaps matters most is why we make the choice. We can rest in order to handle responsibility better or simply out of self-indulgence or rebellion. We can do our duty out of concern for others, or out of self-righteousness. Here I find no easy answers, no infallible tests we can apply. It seems to be a matter of how honest we can be with ourselves, and we can err as much toward self-condemnation as toward self-justification. It may take a lifetime to sort things out, but a lifetime is precisely what we have to work with. We do not become angels overnight, but a little at a time, in pieces we can handle.

At the center of the whole process, there is a paradox. Swedenborgian theology expresses it very simply, with repeated statements that we are to shun evils "as if of ourselves," but with the recognition that it is the Lord's power alone which is actually effective. This is the very same principle that makes A. A. and the other twelve-step programs work. They require the realization that we are powerless to resist the addiction, and then they require us to resist it, "one day at a time." There is a kind of "giving up" that leads to transformation.

We might do well to recognize ourselves as addicted to our own egos. Like the alcoholic, we have our sober times when we resolve to control our self-concern, and like the alcoholic we keep failing. We go through cycles of repentance and efforts to reform on the one hand, efforts to solve the problem through will power, and lapses into whatever particular form our self-concern takes.

These efforts are absolutely necessary. We cannot discover that we are powerless by reading it in a book. We have to try. We have to give it our best shot. Nothing more surely short-circuits the process than the hidden belief that we could succeed if we really put our minds to it. This lets us cherish the illusion of competence without ever putting it to the test. A. A. talks about "bottoming out" and urges people who live with alcoholics to let this happen.

All this may sound rather grim for an Easter message, but without it, Easter can only be superficial. If the disciples could not have been transformed without the resurrection, it must be remembered that there could have been no resurrection without the crucifixion. The depth of the disciples' despair was the precise measure of their joy. Those individuals who rejoiced in the crucifixion found no joy in the resurrection.

So in a sense, the Easter message is measured out to us according to our needs. The central message is clear and simple. The gift the Lord would give us is the gift of spiritual life. He wants us to be at peace with ourselves and with each other. He wants us to go to bed every night with a sense of contentment, and to wake up every morning with anticipation. He wants us to appreciate and enjoy each other. He wants us to know the beauty of a task well done, a word well spoken. He wants us to see the beauty latent in all his creatures and all his creation. In short, he wants to resurrect us from our "half-life," from any sense at all that life is a burden to be borne. He wants us to discover that life is a joy to be lived.

He has not been content simply to tell us this; he has shown us. He has led a human life in circumstances like our own. He heard all the messages we hear about looking out for number one. He saw all the subtle opportunities to compromise, to manipulate people to one's own advantage, to rationalize or justify. He felt all the deceptive promises of reward that our world can hold out to us.

Through all this, he lived. He refused to be dulled, deadened by the bleakness of human egotism, in himself or in others. Step by step, he became so alive that physical death itself had no power over him. His whole purpose was to enable us to do the same in our own individual and limited ways. "These things have I spoken unto you, that my joy might remain in you, and that your joy might be full." "If you keep my commandments, you shall abide in my love; even as I have kept my Father's commandments, and abide in his love."

The Palestine of Jesus' time did not have computers or traffic jams, nuclear weapons or television. It did have wars and oppression, slavery and greed; and above all, it did have life and death. Whatever forms our circumstances may take, the central issues are constant. The promise still holds that faithfulness will surely bring peace and joy. "In the world you will have tribulation, but be of good cheer—I have overcome the world." Life is not just bodily processes, it is liveliness, eagerness, engagement. It is what we feel when "life is worth living," and that is how the Lord wants us to feel. "I am come," he said,"that they might have life, and that they might have it more abundantly.

Practical Living

Conventional wisdom sometimes divides people into two classes, the idealists and the realists, the dreamers and the practical people. It isn't that simple. We have all seen contented and successful people who have held fast to their ideals, and we have all seen hard-headed "realists" whose lives have come apart on them. There is an immense amount of wisdom on this subject in the Gospels, and I'd like to look at some of it. Most of it will be familiar, but it may help to bring it together.

Right at the center of the issue is Jesus' very familiar admonition from the Sermon on the Mount:

> Lay not up for yourselves treasures upon earth, where moth and rust doth corrupt, and where thieves break through and steal; but lay up for yourselves treasures in heaven, where neither moth nor rust doth corrupt, and where thieves do not break through nor steal: For where your treasure is, there will your heart be also.
>
> (Matthew 6:19–21)

This is not an easy saying to live up to. We tend to think of practical people as "down-to-earth," and if we call someone "other-worldly," we usually mean that person is not very practical. So before we gloss over the difficulties, we need to recognize that this saying is not advising us to pay no attention to worldly matters. It is telling us not to set our hearts on them.

Let's take an example. We want safety and comfort for our families, and work hard to live in safe and comfortable surroundings. If possible, we buy a house in a neighborhood where people share our basic values, a neighborhood where we can feel at home. There is nothing wrong with this. But if we think that the house is going to make us feel safe and comfortable, we are setting ourselves up for disillusionment. If we are not working to be at peace with ourselves, then we will not be at peace with our families, and when there is anger breaking out in the home, before long we will not be at peace with our neighbors.

Or let's take a parable instead. Suppose you were building your home rather than buying it. Anyone with an ounce of practicality would tell you to use materials that will last. You can do a quick and cheap job that may even look elegant, but if the paint is going to peel and the sills are going to rot and the shingles are going to crack, you've wasted your money disastrously. Every once in a while we read about someone who has gotten stuck with a badly-built house, and it is a horror story of mounting expenses for something that is next to worthless.

Jesus is saying that in comparison with spiritual, heavenly realities, the whole physical world is like that. Compared to our souls, our bodies just won't last. Compared to our qualities of mind and heart, our physical houses are strictly temporary. Compared to our talents and our abilities, our bank accounts are definitely short-term. Let's face it, we are going to have to live with ourselves forever, and it makes all kinds of sense to try to be people we can stand to live with.

Make no mistake about it, though. The means by which we become people we can live with are right here in the physical world. We become honest and trustworthy by building solid houses, by using our money responsibly, by keeping our commitments. We become gentle and compassionate by taking care of people with our words and our deeds—by helping those in need and in distress. In Swedenborg's terms, a spiritual character has to be built on a physical foundation. It isn't a castle in the air. The point of the Sermon on the Mount is that the physical, necessary as it is, is not the goal, is not an end in itself, but a means. If we perform a useful service for someone who needs it, our action is inadequate unless it arises from and encourages a genuine caring for that individual.

It is a prime case of both/and rather than either/or. We need both the compassion and the action. If we stop and reflect on the last decade or so of our country's history, it seems as though there was a massive effort to believe that everyone could take more out of the system than they were putting into it. The heroes were the people who had found ingenious ways to get rich rather than the people who had found ways to do something worthwhile or had actually done something worthwhile.

These were the so-called "practical" people, the ones who thought we could build a thriving economy simply by stimulating everyone to get as much out of it as possible. This is where the hard-nosed idealist needs to come in and point out the obvious fact that if you pump more out of the well than is flowing in, the well is going to run dry. Grown-ups can figure out theories complicated enough to pretend it isn't so, but it is obvious to most children.

If "laying up treasures on earth" is the goal, though, it is unwelcome news. Of course we need to work for financial security. Again, Swedenborg says quite explicitly that we cannot be of much use to the neighbor if we are in need of everything ourselves. But as we tend to our physical and financial needs, our hearts need to be set on such spiritual goals as integrity, understanding, and mutual affection. These will last forever—and so, it seems, will their opposites.

Together with this, we might also look at the parable of the talents. The obvious message of this is that we must use whatever gifts we have been given, but there is a kind of by-product as well. That is the message that it is pointless to compare ourselves with others. It is not a matter of who has more or less to work with, but of what we are doing with what we turn out to have. There may be a certain amount of emotional validity to sentences that begin, "If I were you," but we must not let them delude us. The fact is that I am not you and never will be, so rather than trying to figure out what kind of you I would be, I had better concentrate on deciding what kind of me I want to be.

This carries over into matters of circumstance, to sentences that begin, "If I were in your shoes." No one could accuse Helen Keller of social irresponsibility. She was a tireless worker for the unfortunate. Yet she wrote,

> Now I am as much up in arms against needless
> poverty and degrading influences as anyone else,
> but, at the same time, I believe human experience
> teaches that if we cannot succeed in our present
> position, we could not succeed in any other. . . .
> The most important question is not the sort of en-
> vironment we have but the kind of thoughts we
> think every day, the kind of ideals we are follow-
> ing; in a word, the kind of men and women we re-
> ally are. The Arab proverb is admirably true: "That
> is thy world wherein thou findest thyself."

If we use this as an excuse for evading our social responsibilities, that is saying something very dark about "the kind
of thoughts we think every day, the kind of ideals we are following; in a word, the kind of men and women we really
are." If we refuse to face its wisdom, though, then we delude
ourselves into thinking we have done much more than we
really have when we provide material help to someone in
need. We offer enduring help only when, so to speak, the
gift of food is accompanied by the gift of understanding and
affection. Sometimes what is needed is that difficult quality
currently known as "tough love"—the refusal to bail out
which impels the other to accept responsibility. Without
understanding and affection, we do not know when it is
right to say yes and when it is right to say no.

A similar message is conveyed by the story of the
widow's mite. We cannot judge the spiritual value of an act
by its price tag in dollars. There are laws specifically designed to encourage charitable gifts, and people can develop such skills in the use of those laws that companies

and individuals can make substantial donations and come out ahead. We can surely be grateful to discover that such and such a company has set up a foundation which is doing wonderful things, but the parable is telling us that our own apparently minute efforts may be qualitatively greater. Incredible as it seems, the evening you spend at the soup kitchen, or the time you spend getting clothes ready for Goodwill, may amount to more spiritually than the annual program of the Ford Foundation.

Now that really sounds like an ivory-tower sentiment, but it needs to be taken seriously. What Jesus is saying goes back to something eminently practical, namely that our outward problems have their roots in our attitudes toward each other, and that the problems will not be cleared up until those attitudes change. Oh, we may solve this problem or that one, but unless we as people become more consistently humane, the same inhumanities will simply break out in new forms. A scholar named Samuel Kramer wrote a book called *It Happened in Sumer: Twenty-one Firsts in Recorded History*. He takes texts four thousand or more years old, and the people are awfully recognizable. There's a first case of apple-polishing, a first case of teenage delinquency, and so on. It seems as though human nature hasn't changed all that much.

This would be immensely discouraging if it were not for one absolutely vital fact. We know that human nature can change. We have seen it happen, in ourselves and in others. We can look back on our own lives and see that we have learned greater sensitivity and understanding. We can read stories of people who have awakened to new senses of responsibility and mission. Perhaps we can even suspect

206

that this would happen more often if we paid more attention to it, if we valued such growth more highly, if we were more concerned to lay up for ourselves treasures in heaven.

Our Lord's kind of idealism is severely practical. He is urging us to look deeply and honestly at what really works, at what really increases our sense of peace and wholeness. The Gospels are not just pretty stories about how everything will be nice if we are nice. They are strong stuff, designed to shatter some of our cherished illusions—illusions about how happy we would be if only we had this or that, illusions about how much better we are going to be tomorrow, illusions about how our problems are really someone else's fault. They press us to face reality—the spiritual reality that is so real that it lasts forever.

What's Happening?

The main premise for my theme is well presented in *True Christian Religion* n. 475f., and I'd like to start by quoting it at some length.

> As long as we are living in the world, we are kept in between Heaven and Hell where there is a spiritual balance which is our freedom of choice.
>
> If we are to know what our freedom of choice is and what its nature is, we need to know where it comes from. Acquaintance with its origin is the primary resource for recognizing not only what it is, but also what it is like. Its source is the spiritual world, where the Lord keeps our minds.
>
> Our mind is our spirit, which lives on after death. Our spirit is in constant association with like spirits in that world; and through the physical body that envelops it, it is in association with other people here. The reason we do not know that mentally we are surrounded by spirits is that our associate spirits are in the spiritual world. They are thinking and speaking spiritually. We, in contrast, think and speak naturally as long as we are in our

bodies. Spiritual thought and speech cannot be understood or even perceived by natural people, nor is the reverse possible. As a result, they cannot even see each other.

However, when our spirit is in the company of spirits in their world, then it is involved in spiritual thought and speech with them, since our more inward mind is spiritual, even though our more outward mind is natural. So we communicate with them through these more inward levels, and communicate with each other through our more outward ones.

This deeper communication enables us to perceive matters and think them through analytically. If we did not have this communication, our thinking would be no more than and no different from that of animals. In fact, if this interaction with spirits were cut off, we would instantly die.

A few words are in order to enable us to understand how we are kept in between heaven and hell, and therefore in the spiritual balance which gives us our freedom of choice. The spiritual world consists of heaven and hell. Heaven is above the head, and hell is below the feet—not in reference to the planet where we are dwelling, but in reference to the lands of that world, which, being of a spiritual origin, are apparently extended but not actually extended.

Between heaven and hell there is a vast interspace, which looks like a whole world to its inhabitants. Evil breathes full force into it from hell, and good, also in full force, breathes into it from heaven. This interspace is what Abraham was describing to the rich man in hell: There is a great gulf fixed between us, so that those who want to cross from here to you cannot, nor can any cross from you to us. (Luke 16:26)

Every one of us is in this interspace as to the spirit, solely so that we may have freedom of choice.

Since this interspace is so vast, and seems like a great world to the people who live there, it is called the World of Spirits . . . .

From infancy to old age, we are all changing our locations or places in that world. . . . We are not in this interspace or middle area physically, but spiritually, and as we change state spiritually, tending toward good or evil, we are moved to a location or site in one region or another, and come into association with the spirits who live there. It must be known, though, that the Lord does not move us around—we move ourselves in our various ways. If we choose the good, then a transfer toward the East is effected by us, with the Lord (or better, by the Lord, with us); if we choose the evil, then a transfer toward the West is effected by us, in cooperation with the devil (or better, by the devil, in cooperation with us). We need to note that when we refer to heaven in these pages, it means the Lord, since the Lord is the All in everything of heaven; and when we refer to the devil, it means hell, since everyone there is a devil.

This is a relatively straightforward description, with extensive implications. Let me list a few of those implications, just to get us started. First of all, this world is not like heaven and not like hell. It is a meeting ground of the two, and there will be good aspects and bad aspects to everything we experience. Second, there is a whole level of life of which we are not conscious. Third, our own choices between good and evil have consequences on that level. Fourth, we are not "independent" creatures: even when we are physically alone, we are inwardly in the company of others. Fifth, when we die, we will lose consciousness of this world and come into consciousness of the spiritual environment in which we have been living all along.

I want to focus on the third of these implications, that our present choices have consequences on a level of which we are not aware. Swedenborg states very clearly that the physical cannot be conscious of the spiritual, which means that we cannot see clearly what we are doing to ourselves. We cannot see the kinds of spirits we are choosing to associate with.

As a result, we may be prey to anxiety about our lot after death. I suspect that most of us, even though intellectually we know better, still resort to "balance-sheet thinking" in this regard. We probably do not do this in terms of actions, trying to figure out whether our good ones outnumber our bad ones, but we are likely to do it in terms of our traits. You know the sort of thing I mean. "I'm pretty responsible, but I do have a temper," or "I'm generally considerate of others, but I do procrastinate." On a deeper level, we realize that even our best intentions seem to be tinged with concern for ourselves, and we don't know just how selfish we are.

In one sense, Swedenborg doesn't offer us much help

with this problem. I think, though, that he makes this kind of thinking irrelevant. We are going to wind up precisely where we want to be. There may be some surprises, though. There will certainly be some if we have made a practice of deceiving ourselves, which we can do quite successfully.

Swedenborg also gives us a good deal of information about what this inner world is like and how it works. So while only our own honesty can tell us what we really want, our minds can grasp what works spiritually and what doesn't. At one point, Swedenborg uses a nice comparison which may help at this point. He compares entering the spiritual world with arriving in an unfamiliar country. When we do this, we need to find out what the laws of that country are, so that we know how to behave. Clearly, this does not guarantee that we will behave ourselves; it means only that we will know how to.

In a very similar way, knowing how the spiritual world works, knowing what its laws are, does not guarantee that we will live any better. It does mean that we know how to.

Perhaps the most obvious difference between that world and this is that in a spiritual world, there are no secrets. "Externals correspond to internals." The whole process of judgment after death is simply the process of bringing externals into accord with internals, so that we do and say what we really mean. That, plus the removal of everything that opposes our "ruling love," our primary goal, is the essence of the judgment process. From then on, it is just a matter of our own moving toward the people who are most like ourselves.

Now remember the *True Christian Religion* quote we

began with. That moving is going on right now. We are deciding what kind of people we want to be, and therefore what kind of people we want to be with. Physical circumstances may bring us into the company of different kinds of individuals, some welcome and some not. But right now, we are inwardly remote from spirits who do not share our values, and inwardly close to ones who do.

There is another very important aspect to this. Right now, there are no secrets inwardly. The deeper our thoughts, the truer they are. The only way we can deceive ourselves is to think superficially, to concentrate on appearances. When we do this, we set ourselves at war with ourselves, because deep down inside, we know.

I used to wonder why Swedenborg says that evil always tends toward externals. It certainly seems as though some evils go pretty deep, and as though some people are pretty deeply malevolent. But this, according to Swedenborgian theology, is a relative depth only. It involves, in technical terms, the depths of the natural, and does not reach into the spiritual. In fact, it closes the spiritual off; and one of the most frequent images Swedenborg uses to describe the process of regeneration is the image of "opening the internals."

It now seems to me as though a primary reason evil tends toward superficiality, toward externals, is that only on that level is deception possible. When we are at our worst, evil seems good to us. It is a familiar principle.

For all of us, the good is what brings pleasure to our affection, and the true is what therefore brings delight to our thinking. So we all label "good" whatever we feel as pleasant, from the love of our intentionality; and we label "true" whatever we therefore perceive as delightful, from the wisdom of our ability to discern. (*Divine Providence* n. 195 [2])

In *Tiger in the Smoke*, Margery Allingham wrote, "'Evil, be thou my good.' That is the only sin from which there is no salvation, because when it has completed its work with you, there is nothing left to save" (quoted from memory). We might also say that there is no salvation from this life decision because we have redefined salvation to suit ourselves, and we get precisely the salvation we look for.

Now, evil is not good. In order to believe that it is, we have to engage in a major effort to distort the facts. We set ourselves at odds with reality itself and have to make up explanations of everything that would prove us wrong—which in the last analysis, is everything there is. We have to restrict ourselves to that outermost level of thought where appearances reign supreme, where things are not necessarily what they seem. We cannot for a moment afford to look beneath the surface, where things appear as they are.

In other years, I have explored this idea at greater length, noting that it involves good news and bad news. The bad news is that there are things within us that we do not want others to know, so the thought of "having no secrets" can be threatening. The good news is that hiding from others is both difficult and lonely, and there is something immensely appealing about not having to pretend any more.

The news I want to emphasize this is that there is within each one of us a level at which we are incapable of pretense. There is a level that is absolutely genuine, a level where we see clearly. Swedenborg puts it this way:

> By birth, we are all gifted with the ability to discern
> what is true even to that deepest level where an-
> gels of the third heaven are. . . . So we can become
> rational as our discernment is raised. . . . If the love
> of our intentionality is not raised at the same time,
> then no matter how high our discernment's wis-
> dom may rise, it eventually falls back to [the level
> of] its love.
>
> *Divine Love and Wisdom* n. 258

Swedenborg knew this from experience. He writes about meeting people in the spiritual world who had been relatively ignorant during their physical lives, but who, because they were loving individuals, came into angelic wisdom after death.

This should help us to a saner definition of intelligence than the one we usually assume. What we usually regard as intelligence is at best the ability to express what we know. That is a useful ability, which we should all cultivate in our individual ways. We should not, however, confuse it with the ability to know, or as the *Divine Love and Wisdom* quotation puts it, "the ability to discern what is true." We all have this ability. We all have angelic brilliance of mind. We certainly vary in our ability to express what we discern, and we apparently vary in our access to that level of knowing.

I suspect that this accounts for a number of things, among them the power of positive thinking. Negative thinking tends to deny that this ability exists, and therefore hinders access to it. Experiments have been done with children which demonstrate strikingly how strongly a teacher's expectations influence a child's performance. Teachers were given falsified reports about last year's grades, and the supposedly bright ones wound up improving markedly over the previous year, while the grades of the supposedly slow ones dropped. Once the actual reports were made available, the results reversed themselves.

I suspect also that education would be vastly improved if it were based less on the assumption that everyone should learn the same things, and more on a profound curiosity about the unique potential of each child. It has been amply demonstrated that different people have different "learning styles"—some more visual, some more auditory, some more verbal, some more pictorial. But we still have a lot to learn about learning, and I can think of no better premise for educators than Swedenborg's assumption of an indwelling angelic intelligence.

We began with the quotation from *True Christian Religion*, focusing on the implication that there are inward consequences to our life decisions, and there is one more aspect of this that I should like to close with. It involves particularly the aspect of spiritual companionship, coupled with the principle that our thoughts and affections reach out around us (see *Heaven and Hell* n. 203).

I think it is pretty obvious that we are influenced by what other people think. We may like to believe that we make up our own minds about everything, but the fact remains that we "make them up" out of available material. We live in an environment of ideas. We participate in that environment. It can be difficult for us to understand how people from other cultures think, primarily because it is difficult for us to think in ways our culture does not affirm or practice.

This is one reason why churches—and nations—keep turning to parochialism. In its own way, it works. Participants come to believe genuinely that the world is what the group believes it is. This does not happen solely by deliberate teaching, but by the far stronger and subtler power of shared assumptions.

I would suggest that the more deeply we trust in the actual truth of Swedenborg's writings, the less likely we are to resort to parochialism. Swedenborgian theology puts a high premium on "the affection for truth"; and I am convinced that to interpret this as a love of the writings themselves is a serious distortion. I believe the affection for truth that Swedenborg is talking about manifests itself primarily as a constant effort to figure out what is really going on, to see things from as many sides as possible, to see through our own deceptions. There is a significant difference between believing that something is true because Swedenborg said so and believing that Swedenborg said something because it was true.

Put this together with the extent to which our thinking is shaped by our culture, and the only sane course is a very non-dogmatic one, rejoicing in the fact that other people see things differently, recognizing that wherever we turn our attention, the Lord is there, and there is something for us to learn.

Facing Violence

There is nothing new about violence. When I was in my teens, I knew an elderly woman whose voice would crack uncontrollably. I learned only a couple of years ago that this was because she had been hit in the throat by her father when she was a child. It had happened in a small New England town, and probably everyone knew about it, but no one talked about it. But that is recent history. We can look back and back and back, and find violence sometimes glorified, sometimes taken for granted as a way of life, but never far away. The Bible has images of violence in the time of Noah, when "the earth was filled with violence," and in fact sets the first murder, the first instance of domestic violence, in the second generation of the human race.

We would not take this literally, but the import is still clear. The picture we are given is that violence has been resident in the human heart since very early in our history. I want to spend our time first trying to understand this in the light of Swedenborgian theology, and then looking at some very down-to-earth things that we should be doing.

The first and in some ways most important point is that

we tend to resort to violence when we are afraid. It is not just a matter of something called "anger," but of anger with the specific component of fear. It might seem as though there could be no fear on the part of the abusive parent or husband, but this is only a superficial appearance. As children grow in independence, there can be a definite fear on the part of their parents that they will lose control. It might seem as though there could be no fear on the part of a two hundred pound husband facing a one hundred pound wife, but this is only a superficial appearance. To be rejected by a woman can be a mortal blow to a man's self-esteem.

We need, I think, to recognize two factors in violence—inward fragility and outward strength. When we are at peace with ourselves, when we have a sense of inner security, violence has no appeal to us. When we feel threatened, the "flight or fight" reflexes come into play, and we are likely to "fight," to choose violence, only when there is absolutely no alternative or when we believe we are physically strong enough to succeed. Otherwise, the physical fear is likely to outweigh the deeper fear.

There is a very pertinent bit of wisdom in Jeremiah (9:23f.):

> Thus saith the Lord, Let not the wise man glory in his wisdom, neither let the mighty man glory in his might, let not the rich man glory in his riches: But let him that glorieth glory in this, that he understandeth and knoweth me, that I am the Lord which exercise lovingkindness, judgment, and righteousness in the earth: for in these things I delight, saith the Lord.

The basic message is straightforward. All our efforts to impress ourselves and others by our intellectual ability, our physical strength, or our wealth not only miss the point but actually distract us from it. The point is that we are valued by the Lord; and once we become convinced of this, we have no further need of bolstering our egos. We have no inclination to resort to verbal or physical or economic violence, because we are intrinsically secure.

Not only that, we are secure in a Lord whose primary characteristics are lovingkindness, judgment, and righteousness, and we will prize those qualities above all others. When Darwin or his successors portrayed the fundamental law of nature as being the survival of the fittest, and construed this into a kind of "eat or be eaten" philosophy, it marked the formulation of a philosophy of violence. It is only recently that biologists have paid attention to the fact that a species must contribute in order to survive—that the surest road to extinction is uselessness.

Darwin advocated the principle of natural selection because he was looking for a way to account for the facts "scientifically"—that is, in terms of observable causes and effects, without falling back on any notion of purpose or providence. Everything had to be accounted for in terms of the past. One could not say that a particular development happened, say, in order to prepare for the development of human beings.

Swedenborg would not for a moment take the creation account literally. He is far more at home with the notion that creation took a long time, and that the human race came into being gradually. But he would insist absolutely that there was a divine purpose behind the long process—a Lord who exercises lovingkindness, judgment, and righteousness. That is the central question, and in the debates that sometimes break out between scientists and theologians, that is the point that really makes a difference. It is Einstein's question—"Is the universe a friendly place or not?"

It matters, it really makes a difference, because if the universe is not a friendly place, then there is no real reason why we should be friendly. Someone coined the saying, "Just because you're paranoid doesn't mean they aren't out to get you," which catches the point very nicely. If the universe is intrinsically violent, or intrinsically unfeeling, or intrinsically haphazard, then the course of wisdom is surely to grab for whatever we can get when chance offers it to us. If we have to use force, then all we need to do is to make sure that we do not overmatch ourselves. We had better not get caught by anyone or any organization stronger than we, such as the police.

When there is no sense of an underlying benevolence to our world, no sense of a higher purpose to our existence, this is the way things feel. There is a radical insecurity, and in the face of a hostile or uncaring universe, fear is the only sane response. Of course we fight back.

The most obvious forms of this are physical, and here men have, by and large, a decisive advantage over women, and adults a decisive advantage over children. It is estimated, for example, that in this country, every fifteen seconds a woman is struck by her husband or partner. That is four every minute, or some forty since I began talking. The number of children who suffer physical abuse is equally appalling, and here the mothers do not emerge as blameless.

We need also to be aware, though, that verbal violence can devastate a child's spirit as surely as physical violence. I suspect all of us have seen parents speak to children in public in ways that made us wince. There are adults who still cannot believe that they are intelligent or that they are worth anything at all because they were told over and over again that they were stupid or worthless. There are people who believe, deep down inside, that it would have been better if they had never been born, because they have been told so.

What does Swedenborgian theology say? It says that every individual who is born is designed by the Lord. If we cannot see the purpose for that individual, it is because we are not very good at seeing. It says that we should be trying to see, trying to discover what the Lord has in mind. In doctrinal terms, "The good in the neighbor is the neighbor to be loved." We do not understand anyone until we begin to glimpse the distinctive "good" within.

Fundamentally, though, we are told that we are profoundly interdependent creatures. We need each other, and our lives will become richer as we let go of our efforts to control everything and trust the Lord first of all and then each other. This is no blind or naive trust, no denial that people can be untrustworthy. It is rather the firm faith that in the struggle, the strongest force is goodness. The more real the Lord's lovingkindness, judgment, and righteousness become to us, the greater is our sense of security, the less we are prompted by fear, and the less likely we are to resort to violence, whether physical or verbal.

This thought may serve as a kind of bridge to the down-to-earth things I promised to end with. The very first is to carry into our lives this recognition that outward violence is a sign of inward insecurity and fear. People who are inwardly secure, people who have an abiding sense of their own worth in the Lord's sight, are not inclined to violence. So in dealing with any violence we meet in others, or in ourselves, the first question we need to ask is, "What is the threat?" What is this other person, or what am I, trying to ward off?

That, I think, is an absolutely necessary approach if we are not to wind up meeting violence with violence. Still, it is only part way "down to earth," and I should like to get more specific.

The victims of violence are often afraid or ashamed to tell anyone or to ask for help. This means that if anyone does say or even hint that he or she is a victim of domestic violence, we should take it very seriously indeed. We may know the person who is being suspected of violence as a charming and delightful individual in public, but we must not let that persuade us to forget about the whole thing. For every non-victim who claims to be a victim, there are probably hundreds of victims who remain silent.

If we have anything to do with children, we should be alert to unexplained injuries or absences. Again, it is very unlikely that the child will admit that there has been abuse.

Third, we should become familiar with the resources our communities have to offer, which range from the obvious one of the police through various social services to shelters for battered women and programs run by churches. The issues in any individual case are complex, and situations are likely to be explosive. Our own amateur efforts to help may do more harm than good.

It is no light matter to call a social agency and say that

we have reason to suspect some form of domestic violence. Usually, the wisest course of action when dealing with an adult is to encourage and support the adult to get professional help. If we are dealing with a child, some kind of reporting may be the only avenue open, and then it becomes absolutely vital to stick strictly to the facts—this is what we observed and when we observed it. An unfounded accusation can play havoc with the life of an innocent person.

Strange as it may seem, we may be grateful that our society is beginning to pay attention to domestic violence. What we do in our private lives makes a great deal of difference to those nearest to us; and here above all, our religion should be our guide.

Out of the Depths

The Book of Psalms has been a rich resource for the devotional lives of both Jews and Christians, and the reason is not far to seek. For the most part, the Psalms are not stories or laws, but mood pieces, and they cover a wide range of feelings. We do have our ups and downs, times when we are on top of the world and times when life seems almost unbearably bleak; and there seems to be a psalm that catches the spirit of every occasion.

I want to focus on the down times, not to leave the impression that this is all there is to life, but because this is when we most need help. There is a substantial literature about "depression," which testifies both to its frequency and to its importance. It may help simply to realize that the Bible knows about it too. This is not a book that sees life through rose-colored glasses, not a book that is all sweetness and light. The story tells of tragedy as well as triumph, of the destruction of Jerusalem as well as the building of the temple. It tells the story of the crucifixion as well as that of the transfiguration, prophesies troubles as well as salvation. Psalm after psalm portrays the suppliant as overwhelmed and pleading for rescue. "Out of the depths have I cried unto thee, O Lord." "My life is spent in grief, and my years with sighing." "I am troubled; I am bowed down greatly; I go mourning all the day long." "I am a worm, and no man; . . . I am poured out like water . . . : my heart is like wax; it is melted in the midst of my bowels."

We have all been there. We have all had times of profound and pervasive discouragement, when it was hard to believe that it was all worth it. Circumstances play a part in such passages, but by no means the only part. There have been times when everything was going wrong at once, and we found ourselves challenged and energized, ready to go out and take on the world. There have also been times of depression when we could not identify any particular cause, when nothing was unusually wrong. Sometimes, in fact, it seems that depression is touched off by the very ordinariness of life itself. We seem to be doing the same thing day after day after day, and suddenly, for no apparent reason, it gets to us. Nothing in our circumstances has changed, and that is precisely the problem.

When we turn to Swedenborgian theology, we do not find the words "depression" or "discouragement" in the concordance, because these were not popular terms when the translations were made. We find an abundance of information, though, under words that are not currently in style—under "despair," "desolation," and "vastation." In fact, Swedenborg sees the religious life not as a state of bliss but as a process of growth, and over and over again he insists that the "down times" are a vital aspect of that process. He calls attention to the fact that Jesus knew times of despair as well as times of exaltation, and he finds this central to this epochal meeting of the Divine and the human.

We might take just a few moments to look at this more closely. Swedenborgian theology portrays Jesus as inwardly divine and outwardly human from conception. In his times of deeper consciousness, he identified with the divine so strongly that he could speak of being one with the Father. When his consciousness moved to the more outward aspects of his being, he felt alone and lost, and prayed to the Father as a distant Being. By faithfulness in these latter states—in his times of depression, we might say—he gradually enabled the inner Divine to fill the outer human, so that by the end of his life, the human was wholly "glorified" or made divine.

Swedenborgian theology sees us as set in a very similar situation. We are not described as inwardly divine, true, but we are sustained in life through an "inmost" where the Lord is directly and wholly present. Life flows into us through that inmost center, and from there it flows out through the depths of our being into those outward levels where we live our conscious lives. From our point of view, impulses "arise," thoughts "occur," and feelings "well up." From a more theological point of view, the Lord's love and wisdom are flowing out from within, taking the particular forms that our humanity and our circumstances offer.

There is always more to us that we can be conscious of. But our consciousness, like that of the Lord, does not sit still. It also moves in and out, to higher and to lower levels. We might say that we experience ourselves a little at a time. The trouble is, perhaps, that we tend to get so involved in each particular experience that we assume it is telling us the whole truth. We really are wonderful and special, or we really are worthless, the "worms" of the psalmist.

It may help to bring in another Swedenborgian thought here, namely that each of us is a miniature image of the whole. That is, we can look at something like a city and find ourselves reflected in it. If we pursue this image just a little way, then we can suppose that we have a kind of central government, that we have various areas of particular interest, like different businesses, and that we have ways of getting from one to another, like streets. We can also suppose that we have some slums—some parts of our being that are unkempt and in poor repair.

We would prefer not to visit these areas, but unless they are tended to, they will simply get worse and worse and larger and larger. So the Lord's providence leads us into them from time to time, and when this happens, it is because there is work that needs to be done. We tend not to learn very much or to grow very much when everything is going smoothly for us. The most substantial learning and growth happen when we face difficulties, and "depression" is, in a way, the essential spiritual "difficulty."

If we follow up the leads in Swedenborg's use of the word "despair," they lead us to the word "temptation"—specifically, to "spiritual temptation." Usually, I suspect, we think of temptation as being the urge to do something wrong, but from the point of view of Swedenborgian theology, that is a relatively superficial form. The deeper temptations are those times when it seems as though the Lord is absent. If we recall that our very life is the Lord's love and wisdom flowing into us, then this is exactly what is being said in Matthew 24:12, "the love of many shall wax cold." This is how the Lord's apparent absence feels to us.

230

We may take this, then, as one lesson we can learn from depression. This is what I would be like all the time, if it were not for the Lord's presence. It is an illusion that I am cheerful or helpful or intelligent or capable or good in my own right. All these things are gifts, and when I find myself removed from them, I have no power whatever to create them for myself. I remember vividly an elderly woman telling me of a dream in which she was at the bottom of a pit and did not have the strength even to ask for help. This is so central a fact about our natures that it may be misleading to refer to it as a "lesson." It is not something we can learn from a book, that we can memorize and repeat. It is something that must be experienced to be believed, and the experience is by definition depressing.

How necessary is it? It is so necessary that Swedenborgian theology tells us that even angels have their darker days. They too may come to take their blessedness for granted or to feel that it is really "theirs." The very presence of such feelings begins to cut them off from the Lord and brings on the darkness. If we could see deeply enough into our own processes, we would probably discover that our own times of depression have been preceded by similar feelings of self-satisfaction, more or less subtle depending on our own individualities.

We can also learn from depression that there are areas of our being that need attention. There is more to us than meets the eye—even our own eye—and there are aspects of ourselves that we tend to neglect. We would rather live in the well-tended suburbs of our being and forget about the slums. This too is not something we can learn adequately from books. There is no substitute for going there and seeing for ourselves, and it is appropriate that we become immersed in the experience.

Lastly, how can we handle depression? If we take the view suggested by Swedenborgian theology, I think the answers are fairly clear. First of all, we need to exert whatever strength we have to remain faithful, and whatever the appearance, the Lord is present and ready to help. In more everyday terms, we should not take our depression out on others either by treating them harshly or by neglecting our responsibilities to them. And for a truly practical suggestion, there is one simple thing we can do. We can actually tell people that we are depressed. We don't need to give reasons, which is a good thing in view of the fact that we often don't know why we are depressed.

Second, we can know at least mentally that this state is telling us something true but not the whole truth. We can better endure immersion in our slums if in the back of our minds we know that there are resources elsewhere that can be brought in to help. And this underlies the third, and perhaps the most important thing we can do. That is, we can look squarely at the view of ourselves and the world that we are being offered. We can stop trying to pretend that everything is fine, we can stop trying to put all the blame "out there" on a rotten world, we can recognize and reject all the evasions that may occur to us and face the fact that we need help .

When this really sinks in, both the cause and the need of depression are gone. We do not control its departure any more than we control its onset, but it does lift. We find ourselves feeling better again, probably without really knowing why. We begin to be aware of more of the good things in and around us.

This leaves us with one last responsibility, to remember where we have been. It is all too easy just to be grateful that we are feeling better and to start taking things for granted again. But if Swedenborgian theology is right, this is the surest way to set ourselves up for another trip to the slums. Here again, we might well take our cues from the Psalms— "I will extol thee, O Lord; for thou hast lifted me up. . . . O Lord my God, I cried unto thee, and thou hast healed me. O Lord, thou hast brought up my soul from the grave: thou hast kept me alive, that I should not go down to the pit."

Modern Motherhood

For very good reasons, we take a great deal for granted. At the moment, for example, we are presumably unaware of all the physical processes that are essential to our remaining alive. We are not thinking about the labor that went into the design and construction of this building, or of the quarry workers, lumberjacks, textile workers, metallurgists, inventors, and transportation workers, or of the people who raised and educated them—there is simply no place to stop. We take a great deal for granted because if we didn't, our minds would be instantly and constantly overloaded.

If we always took things for granted in this way, though, there would be little fundamental change. We would simply accept everything the way it is. As it is, from time to time people ask questions about the way things are. Often, it is because something goes wrong, and we are impelled to look for solutions, for a better way to do things. Sometimes it seems to spring from pure curiosity, true, but if we look beneath the surface, we normally discover some discontent, however vague, with the status quo.

The questions that arise often seem disturbing. We have learned to cope with established patterns of relationship. We have become insensitive to their drawbacks and accept them as necessities. Changing the patterns takes effort and involves risk. There is no guarantee that the new way will be an improvement, because we do not yet know what its peculiar liabilities may be. A new highway will get us from here to there more quickly, but what will it do to overall traffic patterns and to business, and to the ecology?

But if we look candidly at the world we live in, we cannot avoid the conclusion that the effort and the risk are necessary. We cannot go blindly on doing things the way they have always been done, because there is too much suffering and violence, too much deceit and inequity, to justify that way.

The more basic the pattern that is challenged, the more distressing is the process of change, and in our own days, one of the most basic patterns of all is being questioned—the role of motherhood. A generation ago, it was honored and romanticized. Today it is often portrayed as constricting, as preventing women from realizing their full promise.

It is, I believe, a good thing that these questions are being raised. If that seems a strange statement, it can be put differently—it is a good thing that the role of motherhood is not being taken for granted. None of us likes to be taken for granted. None of us likes to have it assumed that we will do particular things whether we want to or not. Especially when children are small, motherhood is a twenty-four-hour-a-day, seven-day-a-week job, and it is callous to assume that anyone will perform it "of course." It is constricting.

This does not mean that it is necessarily unfulfilling. That depends in part on what we regard as fulfillment. At present, it seems as though our culture defines fulfillment in terms of position, money, and prominence, and on this scale motherhood is a ladder to nowhere. But on a deeper level, the people who succeed in gaining position and money and prominence are not always fulfilled. Many of them lead lonely and empty lives and try to make their prosperity a substitute for a genuine sense of love and joy.

If we look clearly at our lives, it is obvious that our relationships with each other are critical to our happiness. We are most ourselves, most at ease, when we are with people whom we like and who like us. We may have moments when we envy the passenger in the stretch limousine, but the fact is that if we were in it, we would not enjoy it unless we felt welcome.

Central to our happiness, then, are our relationships with people, and that is what motherhood is all about. The relationship between mother and child is extraordinarily close, at times leaving time for little else. The processes of growth and learning from infancy are miraculous. It is ironic that our culture values so highly the people who study these processes, the pediatricians and the experts in child growth and development, and pays so little attention to the people who are involved full-time with the infants themselves.

What is needed is a basic shift in cultural values. We need to become less impressed with technology and with money and more attentive to people for their own sakes. If this were to happen, then motherhood would begin to have the high status it deserves. It would be seen as a high calling, demanding devotion and skill, and leading to personal fulfillment.

This is where the church comes in. When the Lord was asked what the two greatest commandments were, he chose love of the Lord and love of the neighbor. In essence, he was saying that these were the two most important issues in life, and that they were indissolubly linked. Love of the neighbor is central because it is the Creator's own love. It is a matter of national security if you will: our survival depends on it. Without it, we will destroy each other.

It is no coincidence that the Lord is presented as a parent. "When Israel was a child, then I loved him." (Hosea 11:1). Infants in relation to their parents are as powerless as we are in relation to our Lord. Infants and little children may love their parents with all their hearts, but for what seems like a long time indeed, they cannot express that love in actions, they cannot do much to lighten their parents' burdens. As far as actions are concerned, the relationship is a one-way street, with the mother especially doing everything for the infant, and the infant simply receiving the care.

The parents need care as well. We are not sources of life, not the omnipotent creatures we appear to be in the eyes of little ones. We need to know that there is someone supporting us. Beyond that, we tend to model ourselves after those who have power in our lives. Children who are abused tend not only to long for strength to resist, but to see strength solely as a means to violence. As we come to understand something of the Lord's power and love, we begin to see strength as the ability to give and receive, to be constant and reliable. Whatever our failings may be, at least our ideal is human and humane, and we are striving toward it. When Swedenborg writes that our idea of God is the most important idea in our minds, this is one of the things he is implying. The model we have of goodness and power shapes all our decisions.

Swedenborgian theology also insists that love of the Lord must express itself in love of the neighbor. It agrees wholly with the first letter to John: "If a man say, I love God, and hates his brother, he is a liar: for he that loves not his brother whom he has seen, how can he love God whom he has not seen?" If we do actually love the Lord, then we love the qualities that make him who he is, and we reflect in our lives the qualities that we love.

There is one characteristic of that love that is particularly important for motherhood and that deserves special attention in its own right. It is strongly suggested in the last phrase of Hosea 11:1. "When Israel was a child, then I loved him, and called my son out of Egypt." In Egypt, Israel had been slaves. The "calling out" was a call to freedom, to independence, and the feast of Passover is, as far as we know, the original independence day.

What this is saying is that the Lord's love is not the kind that keeps us conscious of our dependence. It is the kind that leads us into freedom. The goal of motherhood is not to keep the children forever, but to help them to grow into adults, to become capable of being parents themselves. The goal of motherhood is to stop being a mother.

This is why it is vital to see motherhood in the context of human relationships. If a woman's whole identity is found in mothering, then when the children are grown, there is little left for her. She is in fact likely to regret the very growth that she needs to encourage, and in subtle ways to try to keep them dependent. The love of children needs to be part of a love of people, and this can happen only if parenting is seen as a specialized form, so to speak, of the most basic human quality. Or to put it negatively, it cannot happen if motherhood is seen as competing with other relationships.

Certainly, motherhood competes for time and for attention. But it has been demonstrated time and again that it need not become a preoccupation. A mother can also be a wife and a friend. The relationship with the infant can awaken deeper affection for all of the Lord's children. It can lead to broader and deeper sympathies, to a more perceptive and constant concern for the quality of the community that surrounds the child and for the world that the child will inherit. It can be a path to wisdom and empathy, a foundation for deeper and more rewarding relationships with adults. In short, it can be a most marvelous path to personal fulfillment, to growth into a fuller humanity.

It is not easy. It demands thought and energy, self-discipline and self-sacrifice. So does every worthwhile enterprise. The woman who chooses a career will find herself faced with very similar demands. They are easiest to bear when we can see the potential rewards and believe in their worth. Motherhood needs support, needs to be widely valued, and that valuing must be strong enough to withstand criticism.

There is a real possibility of benefit, then, in the present critical mood. Its questions should not be dismissed but taken seriously and answered thoughtfully. If this is done, then the institution of motherhood cannot fail to emerge more clearly understood and more deeply appreciated. For it is undeniably central to our survival, both physically and spiritually. It is this relationship that continues the human race, and it is in this relationship that infants are formed into the adults of the coming generation. There is a profound need of a model for this critical role, and the church has such a model in the Lord who cares for each one of us and leads us to our fullest freedom and humanity.

Loyalty

Hear this word that the Lord hath
spoken against you, O children
of Israel, against the whole family
which I brought up from t
he land of Egypt, saying,
You only have I known of all the
families of the earth: therefore I will
punish you for all your iniquities.

Amos 3:1f

I t is a familiar principle of Swedenborgian theology that Scripture often presents us with appearances of truth rather than with truth itself, and this text offers two eminent examples. In the first place, the Lord "knows" all the families of the earth, not just the children of Israel. Divine love is not restricted or conditional; it does not play favorites. In the second place, the Lord never punishes anyone. There is no need to, since transgression is inherently destructive of the transgressor.

If we ask why Scripture uses appearances, there are

two primary and related answers. The first looks to the past and seeks out causes. There are appearances in Scripture because different people have heard the Lord's voice so differently. When we are angry, we hear love as threatening. When we feel guilty, we hear love as punitive. The second answer looks to the future and seeks out purposes. In order to move toward the Lord from where we are, there must be messages that speak to our present states in language that we can understand. There are times when we can be kept safe only through the fear of punishment or the hope of reward. It is for our sakes that the Lord allows Himself to be seen as threatening or promising rather than, more truly, as present and loving.

I should like to focus on the first of the two appearances in the text, though— "You only have I known of all the families of the earth." We are acutely aware that this is a perilous statement. It can lead, and has led, to the most exclusive kind of sectarianism. "We are God's only chosen people, and therefore we have the right to do whatever we choose." "Outside the church, there is no salvation." I once received in the mail a flyer for some books on Christian missions, and the description of one of them made it quite clear that, in the author's view, unless the Gospel were proclaimed throughout the world, millions of people would have no hope of salvation.

"You only have I known of all the families of the earth." The meeting at which the first General Conference of Swedenborgians was formed unanimously adopted the following resolution (among others):

> That it is the Opinion of the Conference, that the
> Doctrines and Worship in the Old Church are
> highly dangerous to the rising generation, inas-
> much as they tend to implant in young people the
> idea of Three Divine Persons, to which is unavoid-
> ably annexed the idea of Three Gods; the conse-
> quence whereof is spiritual death to all those who
> confirm themselves in such an opinion.

Unless one happens to know what Swedenborgian theology means by "confirming oneself in an opinion," this will
be read as stating that spiritual death results from incorrect
theology rather than from the way one leads one's life.

"You only have I known of all the families of the earth."
It may seem clear that this statement occurs because that
was how Israel heard the Lord's love, but what can we say
about its purpose? It is so obviously susceptible to misuse—
can we see a constructive side to it?

I believe we can. The goal to which we are called, the
heaven for which we were created, has a particular kind of
oneness. It is a oneness that depends on the unique individuality of all its inhabitants. In our progress toward that
oneness, we seem to swing pendulum-fashion between focusing on ourselves and focusing on our relationships.
There are times when it is necessary for us to forget ourselves in caring for others, and times when it is necessary
for us to forget others and care for ourselves. If we try to
sustain self-sacrifice without relief or respite, we eventually
drive ourselves to exhaustion.

There are smaller and greater cycles in this regard. Most

of us need a little time to ourselves every day, a quiet time when there are no demands on us. We need our weekly breaks from the full-time job. We need our yearly vacation. Without these, we face a future that seems to hold only endless obligation. With these breaks, we find ourselves refreshed and willing to get back to the task with new energy.

Beyond this, there is a pattern to the cycle of a lifetime. The years of schooling are years of preparation rather than of production. In one sense, then, they are quite self-centered. Willing or not, we are primarily "getting" an education rather than contributing to society. The years of early adulthood involve a much higher level of visible usefulness, but there is still a strong sense of "getting" oneself established. It is difficult to give ourselves freely as long as we feel insecure.

It is in full maturity, in the main, that we can afford, psychically, to attend more to giving than to getting. We can move beyond the need to prove our worth, that is, and do things simply because we see that they need doing.

Until we reach this point, our insecurity is very real and significant. It cannot be argued away or wished away. We may be able to recognize it and allow for it, but it still tinges all our decisions. Supportive friends and companions help, just as unsupportive ones hinder. But deeper than this, we need some feeling that our God is on our side, wholly and without reserve.

The fact is that God is on our side, wholly and without reserve, and is constantly trying to tell us so. The fact is also that we see ourselves as being in competition with others. This renders us essentially incapable of believing that God can be wholly on our side without being against those we perceive as threatening us. So when God says, "I love you constantly and unconditionally," all we can hear is "You are the only one I love."

There are the obvious problems with this that we have already noted. But there are even worse problems with the alternative. If we become convinced, in this state of mind, that the Lord loves those whom we experience as opposing us, then we must rebel against the Lord in order to survive. If we cannot find the strength for this, then life becomes quite hopeless. We experience ourselves as condemned to the extent that we experience our enemies as justified. If they are right, then we must be wrong.

So we find ourselves—assuming the best—restricted to the belief that "God is on our side." "You only have I known of all the families of the earth." Like every other stage of our spiritual growth, this is a state that we must pass through, which means that there will be a time when it is right for us to be there, and that we must not get stuck there.

Institutional religions have a mixed record in dealing with this fact of spiritual life. The set of mind that says, "We are right and they are wrong" builds strong and active organizations. It is understandable, I suppose, that churches tend to be content if their members reach this point and progress no further. In doing so, however, they set themselves at risk. There is always the risk that someone will discover beauty and truth outside the boundaries of the church, and that being still in this set of mind, will decide that if the new is right, then the old must be wrong. But there is the more subtle risk, even the certainty, that the church will isolate itself from the larger community of the good; and none of us, as individuals or as groups, can survive in isolation.

Let us recall that the goal toward which we are directed, the heaven for which we have been created, is in its essence "distinguishably one." That is, what makes it heavenly is a profound unity that can come only when the unique identity of every constituent is prized and nurtured. There is a lovely image in Swedenborg's *Last Judgment* n. 12, where he states that everyone who arrives in heaven contributes to its perfection by providing a new connection between people there.

It is absolutely necessary that we develop our distinct individualities. We cannot become angels simply by imitation or by conforming to some prevalent pattern. We must find out who we are, how we differ, what our own particular gifts are. We are right to resist being pigeonholed, whether by gender or by race or by income or by education or by profession or by nationality. Each of these says something about us, but each inevitably misses the essence, misses a grasp of why the Lord designed each of us in just this particular way.

If we see this development of individuality as absolutely necessary to genuine unity, then there are consequences. Perhaps the most noticeable one is that sectarianism no longer stands simply as the antithesis to ecumenism. It may fall into that role, and in fact it will fall into that role if it is seen as an end in itself. But once we see it as contributing to the clarification and development of identity, then we see it as contributing to the development of unity.

This can make a difference in our own attitudes toward those whose church loyalty strikes us as exclusive. Rather than trying to argue them toward more inclusive views, we can try to be more perceptive in distinguishing the constructive aspects of their loyalty. What is it doing for them? We can be more accurate in resisting the negative aspects, in effect asking them to perfect their loyalty rather than to compromise it.

In a way, this is simply an application of the Golden Rule. We do not want other people to argue us out of the religion we value so highly. We also do not want to let our loyalty take forms that impede others. We are inclined to listen to anyone who can help us live the way we know we should.

Because the Lord is present in every religion, there is a kind of way to the center in every religion that ultimately leads beyond its boundaries. This, I would suggest, is the best way, because it leads most directly to oneness through the path of individuality. It is at our best and deepest that we are most perfectly and beautifully united. Be the best Baptist you can, or the best Muslim or Jew or Hindu or Swedenborgian. Do not compromise your beliefs for the sake of some short-term and superficial agreement. For the best of sectarianism, its good heart and soul, is the fact that the Lord loves you especially in your uniqueness, and once that is known fully and beyond argument, the door to oneness is opened wide.

A Difficult Transition

The transition from Saul to David was a particularly difficult one. Saul was the first king the Isrealite nation had ever had, and he had succeeded in uniting the scattered tribes sufficiently to gain victories over the powerful Philistines. As time passed, though, he proved increasingly unstable, even capricious, and young David grew in popularity.

Saul, in his insecurity, could not live with such a threat to his position, and David soon found himself fleeing for his life. Twice in the course of this flight, he had chances to kill Saul, and both times he refused. As long as Saul was king, Saul was the Lord's anointed, the Lord's Messiah, and David would do nothing to harm him.

As a result, there was a painful period when Saul, in the North, grew increasingly ineffective and alienated, while David, in the South, gained increasing power which he could not really exercise. Even after Saul's death in a defeat, David refrained from making any overt moves. The southern tribes made him their king, but a son of Saul named Ishbosheth was uncontested king of the northern tribes. Only when he was assassinated and the northern tribes came to David did David become king over the entire nation.

There is relatively little in Swedenborg about Saul, but what there is indicates that with Saul, David, and Solomon, we are dealing with a progression from natural to spiritual to celestial. In less technical language, we are dealing with a change of attention from behavior to thought to feeling. Saul is a fitting representative of the attitude that focuses on doing things right. David represents a need to understand what lies beneath the surface of behavior; and Solomon represents an eventual feeling for what is right. I might add that Solomon's decline in his later years indicates that we cannot always trust those feelings.

Here, though, I should like to focus on the transition from Saul to David, the transition from behavioral standards to deeper ones. In one form or another, we are likely to face this transition many times during our lives. Whenever we start a new venture, we have to learn how to do something unfamiliar. We have to acquire new skills, and we become preoccupied with our performance. As we gain the skills, they begin to make sense—we begin to understand why things need to be done in just this way.

This can be an awkward time. I recall a former roommate telling me that his bride had been a marvelous cook until she learned how and started ignoring the recipe books. As we begin to understand, we begin to think of different ways to accomplish the same ends. Sometimes we do come up with better ways. That is how progress is made. Sometimes we come up simply with ways that suit our own circumstances or abilities better. What "works" in the book may not be best for all occasions. Sometimes we may find out the hard way that the book is right. "When all else fails, read the instructions."

But we also face this same transition in more vital areas of life, in our dealings with each other. When we first meet someone, we are likely to notice particularly that individual's behavior. We form a favorable or unfavorable impression based on what that person says or does. If our association lasts long enough, we are likely to discover aspects of the person that are not so obvious. The man who agrees with us politically or theologically may turn out to be self-centered and unreliable. The woman who disagrees with us may turn out to be compassionate and trustworthy.

If we attend exclusively to behavior, to externals, we will discount these deeper facts. "Oh, I know he's hard to live with, but he's got his head on straight." "She may be a nice person, but she doesn't know what she's talking about."

Swedenborgian theology insists that quality is determined by what lies within. Swedenborg even makes the radical statement that the true things an evil person knows are not true, because they are filled with a selfishness that falsifies them. In the same fashion, mistaken opinions that are held honestly and unselfishly can lead us toward deeper and more accurate understanding.

We know from experience the difference between a closed mind and an open one. We can say from theory that until we know all there is to know, a closed mind will be a liability. "Knowing" is actually less significant than "learning," because a heavenly life is a life of growth. This means that we should pay less attention to whether or not people agree with us, and more attention to whether or not they listen to us.

It also means that we should ourselves approach every individual as someone we can learn from. This person may know less than we do, but we can be very sure that this person's knowledge is different from ours. We need to listen before we judge. The old can learn from children. The wise learn from everyone.

One of the areas that is particularly touchy in this regard is the political arena. Our system tends to expect a kind of loyalty to the party line. In a campaign, it seems to be against the rules to admit that one's opponent has any virtues or that oneself has any faults. It is hard to imagine, in a campaign, or in a televised debate, a candidate saying to the opponent, "I hadn't thought of that. That sounds like a good idea."

Yet if we step back a little and think honestly, we know that no one has a monopoly on good ideas. Neither political party is composed entirely of intelligent, dedicated people, and neither party is without intelligent, dedicated people. Neither party always has the answers, and neither party never has the answers.

What I have in mind is a particular application of the Golden Rule, "Do unto others as ye would have them do unto you," and I'd like to try a little mental exercise at this point. First, imagine someone with whom you have a strong disagreement. It may be political, it may be theological—that does not matter for the moment. Then, imagine that individual listening with an open mind to what you have to say. Imagine that individual trying to understand why you feel the way you do, trying to see through your eyes. Imagine that individual admitting that you may actually be right.

Now comes the hard part. Imagine yourself communicating that attitude not by words, but by example. Imagine yourself asking questions not in order to refute the answers but in order to understand better. Imagine yourself assuming that this individual knows some things that you do not know and that you need to know. Imagine yourself actually changing your mind, as you would have the other do.

Then, and only then, do we realize fully what we are asking of the other. Think a moment. Is it fair to ask of others what we are not willing to do ourselves?

This, I would suggest, is the transition from Saul to David. it is the transition, that is, from a partisan judgment on the basis of outward appearances to an inward evaluation; and the inward evaluation is always an evaluation of ourselves as well as of the other, an evaluation by the same standards.

Nicodemus wondered whether this was possible. "Can he enter a second time into his mother's womb, and be born?" Can we become so childlike that we are actually eager to learn? Jesus' answer is unequivocal. "Except a man be born of water and of the spirit, he cannot enter into the kingdom of God."

Intimations

The Bible tells a story. It is a very human story, in which, as in our lives, it is not always easy to figure out what is going on. It is more likely that we can look back after the fact and understand what has happened; and the Bible is of special value because the story carries through to a conclusion, a conclusion which our lives have not yet reached. So wherever we are in the process, we are offered a wisdom, an overview that we may not see while we are caught up in the complexities of our own processes.

The central theme of the Biblical story is a simple one. It is that the Lord is constantly saying, "Come to me," and that we as humans are hearing this in particular ways that depend on our own particular states. Sometimes the call sounds comforting, and sometimes it sounds threatening. Sometimes we hear a call to take arms and fight; sometimes we hear a call to lay down our arms and be at peace. Sometimes our need is to strengthen relationships, and sometimes our need is to be alone for a while.

To use another image, the direction of the Lord's leading is constant, but the terrain we are traversing varies. It is not always uphill and not always downhill; and there are times when the foundation for further progress must be laid during a period of rest. The traffic on the turnpike may have come to a standstill because of an accident three miles ahead, and standing still may seem like no progress whatever. But beyond the range of our perception, calls for assistance have gone out. Emergency vehicles are at work clearing the way. Progress is being made, and every minute brings us closer to our destination—closer in time if not in space.

At such times in our spiritual lives, the message of the Lord is the message of the Psalmist: "Wait for the Lord; wait patiently for him." Suppose, for example, we have reached an impasse in one of our relationships. There is a misunderstanding, and everything we say in the effort to make ourselves clear just seems to make matters worse. We can, figuratively speaking, race our engines and blow our horns, but such actions are ineffective because they are utterly irrelevant. Something is going on that we are not addressing, and we are not addressing it because we do not perceive it.

The signs are there, if we would pay heed to them. There is an edge to our voices, and there is a tension in our bodies. These are parables, physical images of a frustration within, and that frustration stems from an inarticulate recognition of our ineffectiveness. It certainly feels and seems as though we were out of touch with the Lord as our negative emotions rise.

Can the Lord's "Come to me" be heard in these circumstances? Is it taking some form that we do not recognize? Swedenborgian theology answers an emphatic "yes" to both questions. The Divine is constantly and totally present with us, always in the effort to bring us closer to itself. The more negative our state, the more negative will be the terms in which we hear the message.

If we step back a little from the situation we are considering, this may become clearer. Why are we uncomfortable? We are uncomfortable precisely to the extent that we really want to be understood and appreciated. If this longing were not present and active within us, then we would relish the misunderstanding. We would feel secure in our own superiority and welcome every indication of the other's inability to understand us. It has happened from time to time in ecumenical dialogues that just when two parties seemed on the brink of agreement, someone has raised a new objection. The message is clear: "I know that we're right and they're wrong, and I won't be content until they admit it."

I suspect that all of us know what this feels like. We are perhaps particularly susceptible to it because Swedenborgian theology makes such extraordinary claims. But the claims themselves rest on the insistence that the Lord is effectively present within every individual at every moment. If we do not recognize the Lord's presence within that "other," then we cannot see what is going on.

This provides us with our best indication of what to do in such circumstances, namely to face the situation more squarely. There are three simple elements involved. First of all, we need to see clearly that we do want a constructive outcome, and that this is what energizes our sense of frustration. Second, we need to recognize that we are not getting anywhere, and that is the occasion rather than the cause of our discomfort. Third, we need to admit that when we want something and cannot progress toward it, it is because we do not see what the obstacles are.

The third point is the most difficult, and needs a little further explanation. It rests in the basic principle that when love and wisdom are united, the result is effective. It does not mean that we can always find the ideal solution. It may mean only that we can slow down the regress, so to speak. It is a form of progress when we stop making things worse.

So with this in mind, let us return to our situation, the misunderstanding that seems to be getting worse rather than clearing up. There are things we can say. "Something is going on here that I don't understand." "There is clearly something important to you that I can't grasp." "I need some time to think this through, because I don't seem to be able to keep it in perspective." "I have a strong feeling that I'm on the right track, but I must be missing something."

These are only samples intended to be suggestive. The message may take any number of forms, and I certainly would not want to propose that the words be chosen in advance and delivered as a memorized formula. If the recognition is genuine, it will shape the expression to fit the particular situation. The words will carry the nuances that are felt at the time. They will not represent the impersonal exercise of a technique for handling controversy, but an honest and compassionate disclosure of the person.

It cannot be stressed too strongly that the validity of the whole proceeding depends entirely on our hearing the Lord speaking to us through our own thoughts and feelings, speaking to us in parables. This is the absolutely necessary first step toward the larger perspective that makes constructive response possible. We should bear in mind that the Lord did not tell Abram everything that was going to happen. His first call was actually vague in the extreme. "Leave your father's house and go to a land that I will show you." We might phrase this negatively as "This place isn't right for you any more," or in neutral terms as, "Something has to change."

But as Abram followed this first intimation, the messages became clearer. Three chapters after this call, for example, he is told about the future birth of Isaac, and is even told about the eventual bondage in Egypt and the deliverance that will follow. As the story progresses, the promised land is defined with increasing precision, and often there are very specific instructions for particular situations.

We can trust this as an image of the way the Lord's guidance works in our lives. At any given moment, our task is not to straighten everything out. It is simply to hear the Lord's message for that particular situation and to heed it as best we can. If we do, then we can be sure that some next step will emerge in its own proper time. It will involve another set of circumstances, another exchange of messages, another set of inner reactions—a new parable for us to hear and heed.

It may be worth mentioning that real progress in relationships can be made when we are alone. Once the immediate feelings have subsided, once we are under no pressure to respond, we can reflect on what we have said and on what the other has said. We can do this prayerfully, alert to the distorting pressures of self-justification. We can move to a larger perspective, and see what was hidden from us while we were embroiled in the event itself.

This requires a kind of detachment, a kind of suspension of judgment. The first task is to understand, and nothing distorts understanding so effectively as our desire to have things turn out in some particular way. Swedenborg refers to this genuine desire to understand as "an affection for truth" and assigns it a critical role in the process of our regeneration. It means genuinely wanting to know where we have been right and where we have been wrong, preferring the uncomfortable truth to the comfortable illusion.

So to say that "the first task is to understand" may very well mean that the first task is to understand ourselves, to sort out the mixture of inner events that we experience as frustration. In this effort, we must be careful not to get caught in a romantic idealism. There are images of altruism in which it is wrong for us to want anything for ourselves, and such images are dangerous at best and destructive at worst. Swedenborgian theology insists that the only healthy relationship, whether between us and someone else or between us and the Lord, is a reciprocal one. In particular, there are likely to be fairly extended periods in our lives when our primary task is, so to speak, to define ourselves and to declare our independence.

As a kind of corollary to this, we must not allow our effort to understand where we have gone wrong to blind us to the wrongs of others. Others can be all wrapped up in themselves, defensive, resentful, unwilling to move beyond confrontation to mutual understanding. It may well be that we will not move beyond our own frustration until we see this clearly and find ourselves moved with sympathy. We have felt that way, and we know the loneliness and unhappiness involved. Seeing that the impasse was not all our fault, then, can actually contribute to our accepting responsibility for making things better.

All these things Jesus said to the multitude in parables. Everything that we observe with our physical senses comes from some cause or causes on the spiritual level. Those causes leave their traces in what we observe. Our outward experiences are parables, ambiguous representations of what is going on beneath the surface. As we discern the Lord's call within them, we can indeed find our way closer to him.

About the Publisher

During the first half of the 19th century, an itinerant nurseryman named John Chapman criss-crossed thousands of miles planting apple orchards from the Ohio River to the Great Lakes. His unique worldly activity together with a singularly spiritual personality gave genesis to the legends of Johnny Appleseed. The spiritual inspiration for his life's work came to him through his less well-known cargo: the writings of Emanuel Swedenborg. Along with his apple seeds, he deposited Swedenborg books throughout the Midwest for forty years. Sometimes, when his inventory ran low, Johnny would tear a book in half, leaving one part with one farmer and the other with another, and then switch them when he came back through. Nothing gave him greater satisfaction than to discuss and share his "Good News, fresh from Heaven!" Today, we seek to expand the spiritual orchard that Johnny began.

J. Appleseed & Co.

3200 Washington Street
San Francisco, CA 94115

Other Swedenborgian Classics available from J. Appleseed & Co.

———

THE COUNTRY OF SPIRIT, *by Wilson Van Dusen, Ph.D.*
Immediately upon its 1992 release, this volume of selected writings became an instant classic, as Dr. Van Dusen has done once again what he does so well, which is to interpret the depths of Swedenborg's extensive theology and translate it into a compelling approach to spiritual practice for the modern day pilgrim. Included are essays on mysticism, meditation, reincarnation, dream interpretation, and his enormously popular essay on usefulness, plus several others. Exciting reading for the practical seeker.   (132 pages, paperback) $7 postpaid

PRESENCE OF OTHER WORLDS, *by Wilson Van Dusen, Ph.D.*
The leading modern interpretive work on Swedenborg, clinical psychologist and mystic Wilson Van Dusen penetrates the complexities of Swedenborg's singular journey in a way that is helpful particularly for people who are experimental seekers.

> "Here is an account of a scientific genius, dead two centuries, who having mastered all that science knew of the external world, went on to a daring, often frightening exploration of the inner world. Van Dusen, having traveled some of the same distance himself, presents Swedenborg sympathetically in the man's own terms. An exciting, though-provoking book which will appeal especially, I believe, to those persons who are not afraid of the inner psychic world."
>
> —*Carl Rogers, Author and pioneer in humanistic psychology*

(240 pages, paperback. Published by the Swedenborg Foundation) $7 postpaid

To order, please send your check or money order to:
Order Department
J. Appleseed & Co.
3200 Washington Street, San Francisco, CA 94115.
Be sure to specify which books, how many, your name and mailing address.